PARACHUTES POEMS & POLEMICS.

Bernard A. N. Green

Published & Copyright © 2016
Bernard A. N. Green

All rights reserved. No part of this book may be reproduced in any form, by photocopying or by any electric or mechanical means including information storage or retrieval systems, without permission from the copyright owner and the publisher of this booklet.

ISBN 978-0-9576042-1-6

I wish to thank my friend Graham Spicer for helping me with the photographs and formatting of this book. He is admirably suited for this as he is the British Parachute Association Archivist.

FRONT COVER.

This was the poster for British Skydiving Ltd 1964.
In the bottom right hand corner was the office address. There were two versions Thruxton, Aerodrome Nr Andover, Hampshire, and Halfpenny Green, Aerodrome, Nr Stourbridge, West Midlands.

Printed by Biddles Books,
King's Lynn, Norfolk PE32 1SF

CONTENTS

INTRODUCTION 1
DYSLEXIA 2
DYSCALCULIA 2
MUTATIONS 2
DOUBLE DUTCH 3
MY WORD 3
A WORD ABOUT WORD 4
RELEASE, RELIEF, RENEWAL 4
1946-49 6
MALAYSIA 6
A WOMAN I NEVER MET 7
DISAPPOINTMENT 7
BEING STILL IS BORING 8
REMORSE 8

PART 1 PARACHUTES 9

PARACHUTING, 1950's 11
PEACE OF MIND. 11
THE BIG BRA 15
BIG BUM 16
SITTING IN AN OAK TREE 17
MY TIME LINE, PARACHUTING 18

18/SEPT/1960. IRISH PARACHUTING RALLY AT WESTON AERODROME, LUCAN .. 18
B.P.A. TIME LINE, 22/OCT/1960 FORMATION OF THE BRITISH PARACHUTE ASSOCIATION. 19
YOUTH 21
MORNING THOUGHTS 21
SAFE ADRENALIN RUSH.............................21
INTERNET 22
AUTHOR. 22
WHERE'S THE BODY (SKYDIVING).............. 22
BRITISH SKYDIVING CLUB. 27
SKYDIVING IN STYLE. 27
DEADLY COMBINATIONS. Part A. 30
THE WAR LOVER.. 30
PARACHUTING & SKYDIVING...................... 34
SUMMARY.. 35
SKYDIVING AT BIGGIN HILL. 36
BRITISH PARACHUTE ASSOCIATION, ... 40
B.P.A. TIME LINE.. 40
18/SEPT/1960 IRISH PARACHUTING RALLY AT WESTON AERODROME, LUCAN. 43
SUCCESS. 43
THE BRITISH PARACHUTE CHAMPIONSHIPS. 45

iv

THE BRITISH OPEN PARACHUTE CHAMPIONSHIPS. SENIOR EVENT, COMPETITORS 44
WORLD RECORDS 1959-60 44
ABILITY 45
CHAIRS 45
FALLING OUT OVER SHOES (SKYDIVING)... 45
I BLEW IT 49
THE 9 TU 50
PARACHUTE DISPLAYS BY THE BRITISH SKYDIVING CLUB, THRUXTON. 50
DEATH OF MIKE REILLY. 51
MODIFYING AMERICAN CHUTES. 1962 52
B.P.A. 22/APR/1962 52
17th /JUNE/ 1962 PLYMOUTH AIR RALLY. 52
LIVING 53
NHS 53
BRITISH SKYDIVING CLUB 54
MARTIN AND THE PERCIVAL PRENTICE. 54
EVENTS AND DATES 56
DEADLY COMBINATIONS Part B. 58
PARACHUTING & SKYDIVING 58
TRUE PLEASURE 59
BPA. NOVEMBER 1962 CHANGE OF SECRETARY. 60
PARACHUTING (THE SUIT) 60

v

THE FLAT	62
TO VALUE A MAN	63
MOTORBIKE	63
JOY	64
PEOPLES PERSON	64
PALS AND PUBS	64
1/JUNE /1964 BRITISH PARACHUTE ASSOCIATION	65
BRITISH PARACHUTE MAGAZINE	66
SPRING 1965 SPORT PARACHUTIST	66
1966 A FRACTURED SPINE	67
THRUXTON CLUB.	68
ACTIVITY	64
STORMS	69
CHILDREN	69
THE BARRISTER	70
POETIC ATTITUDE	71
BOB ACRAMAN	72
THRUXTON NEWSLETTER.	73
BPA COUNCIL NOMINATIONS.	75
WHALE-BONE	76
MY WIFE KNITTED IT.	76
THE PLACID SEA	82
THE SEA.	83
GIN PALACE	83

SHIPS	83
DREAMS	83
FAME AND SHAME	84
SAD SENRYU	84
BOB ACRAMAN	85
CLOSURE OF BRITISH SKYDIVING LTD	87
SATISFACTION	90
BOB ACRAMAN, THE BUYER	91
THE CHILD	91
TIM BETTIN, THE SKYDIVER	92

PART 2. AUTOBIOGRAPHICAL 93

STORIES AND POEMS	95
THE ENGLISH DAME	95
FARNHAM SURREY	96
THE LANCHESTER CAR	97
PETROL	98
CHERRY BLOSSOM. (Adult)	100
LOVING AND MARRIAGE	101
FELINE FUN	103
THEY SAW WARSAW	103
NAGGING	104
WINTER WOOLIES	105
ARMY DAYS	106

SAPPER GILLFINAN	106
POWER	110
CONSUMPTION	110
DRIVING DINOSAURS	111
SICK AS A DOG	114
NORMANS ABNORMALITY (Adult poem)	115
PROSPERITY	115
MY MOTHER. (Adult poem).	116
IMMIGRATION	116
ILLUSION, DELUSION. (Adult poem)	117
MACKEREL FISHING. (Adult story)	118
JUNK ART	121
1960's HOT & COLD. (Adult poem)	122
HUMOUR. (Adult poem)	123
A MORNING CHAT. (Adult poem)	123
CONTENTMENT	124
MUMBAI. Senryu	124
"THAT'S MA MAN". (Adult story)	125
AUTHOR	129
TWO ODDS MAKE IT EVEN	130
BLOOD RED RAIN	131
ACTING DOPEY	132
BAKING	133
SAUSAGES.	133
PROTECTING PLOD 05/04/2013	136

FINGER NAILS.	137
MESSERSMIT	138
INFORMATION	139
THE GREEN WOMAN	139
THE FUNNY FARM	140
VICARIOUS	143
THE SANDS VILLAGE	144
I KILLED A SPIDER	146
A WAIL	146
BALLOONING STORIES	147
DASHING DAVID	147
A NICE FRIGHT	150
TIME	154
A FLYING BRICK	155
FRESH AIR	159
WIND	159
ALICE'S 80TH BIRTHDAY	160
RELAX	161
AGE	161
THE POT OF GOLD	162
1989 FRENCH BALLOON FESTIVAL.	163
HOT HOUSE	167
EDWARD AND LULU'S NEW BALLOON	168
SOMETHING WRONG ?	172
OLD AGE Three Senru's	172

THE DREAM	173
TO SAVE OR NOT TO SAVE	174
HAPPINESS	175
MEE-JING, TILLS RING	175
GIVING GIFTS	176
PEOPLE POEMS & STORIES	177
PERCEPTION BY PARTICLES	177
HAND WASH	177
BILL THE BAKER 1944. Bill Wilkinson	178
TRAFFIC CONES	179
EBOLA'S REACH.	180
TABOO'S	180
STEVE THE CLIMBER.	181
STEAM PRESSURE	181
CARAVAN by the poet Anaisnais.	182
IT MAKES YOU THINK	182
PERSPECTIVE	183
AUTUMN	185
COLOURFUL LEAVES	185
MARS	186
HOW OLD PEOPLE DISAPEAR	187
FELLING-FALLING-FAILURE	187
CAR DREAMS	188
INTERNET DATING	189
TRAFFIC CONES	189

PHILLISTINE IN PHILLY. (Adult story)	190
DAISIES	194
BREAKING AND ENTERING	195
DYSLEXIC	196
MY PLEASURE	197
A FAULT	197
A GOOD HOUSE FIRE	198
THE MAIL	200
A CARING CARER. My son's carer.	201
DREAMS	202
WHY AM I HERE	203
LOVE CAN CHANGE (Adult).	204
SEEKING PERFECTION	205
BEING OLD	205
PERHAPS.	206
SADLY, KNOW I KNOW.	207
CHINESE FACE	207
LANGUAGE	207
DOUGAL 1998	208
MY BAZOOKA	209
MANKIND.	212
GIVE AND YOU WILL RECEIVE	212
AN ACT OF NATURE	212
IDEAS OF HEAVEN	213
THE DANCING QUEEN.	214

HEY YOU, GOOD LOOKING	215
BATU CAVE	216
ATTITUDE	217
MR DULL	218
THE DIFFERENCE	219
HER ABSENCE	219
ARTIFICIAL INTELLIGENCE	220
GREECE	220
MARRRIED LOVE	220
BLACKIE	221
A NEW VENICE	221
EYE OF THE BEHOLDER	222
LOVE SEX AND MARRIAGE (Adult)	223
BEING GENEROUS	223
MAN, IF SHE COULD BE THE ONE	224
MALFUNCTIONING	226
STRESS.	226
CATARACT	227
A RHYME ABOUT LYME DISEASE.	228
COCKNEY SLANG.	229
POETIC ATTITUDE	230
DEAR-OH-DEAR	231
SWEET FA. A sad story.	232
GROWING OLD	234
THE MONEY MAN	235

KEEPING YOUR MAN OR WOMAN 236

PART 3
NATURE ENVIRONMENT & HUMANITY... 237

TURF WARS 239
THE BARLEY MOW 239
SPRING 240
WHITE LIES 241
HAVE A NICE DAY 242
BE VERY SCARED 243
DREAMS 244
GREECE 244
GREENBACKS AND BROWN PAPER 245
DEAR LEADER 246
FINITE WORLD 246
CARBON TRAILS 247
WATER WARS 247
SIEGE MENTALITY 248
TURF WARS 248
THE POPULATION EXPLOSION 249
SCHOOLING 250
OUR WORLD 250
SNOWFLAKES EQUALS EARTHQUAKES... 251
MONGOL TACTICS 253

EMIGRATION	253
BILLY LIAR	254
YOU CAN ENTITLE THIS	255
NIGHT Senryu	255
PETROL BOMBS. Senryu	255
BOMBS	255
SAVE EARTH ARMY	256
HOUSE AND MONEY	257
LAWRENCE OF ARABIA	257
FEAR	258
BIRTH RATE	258
AFRICAN ANGST.	259
IF WE CAN'T WHY CAN THEY ?	259
PIRATES	260
MORE IS LESS	261
FUTURE	262
THE OVERLOADED DINGHY	263
POWER	264
THE NEW TIBET	264
GRAFFITI	264
OUR WORLD	265
MODERN GOLD RUSH	265
SUICIDE?	265
BREEDING DISCONTENT	266
GROWTH WILL KILL	267

HUMANITY	268
TEARS AND FEARS	269
POLLUTION	269
A PIE IN THE SKY	270
ALL AT SEVENS	271
MORE IS LESS	272
OBESITY	274
SWEET POISON	275
FEEDERS	275
THE COLOSSAL COUPLE	276
BUMS AND TUMS	277
THE WADDLE	278
DREAMING	278
ROLY POLY'S	278
HAIKU-LOVE GIVEN	279
RELEASE, RELIEF, RENEWAL	279
DUST TO DUST	280
BELIEF	280
WINTER	281
THE LAST FLIGHT	281
BEAM ME UP	282
THE LAST PAGE	283
DEATH	284
THE LAST ACT, ON ME	284

INTRODUCTION

I placed some information in my first book called Dunce or Dyslexic about parachuting and Skydiving but the book was in danger of becoming too large. So I have included in this book some more parachuting history also my thoughts on reasons for certain parachuting and skydiving accidents that I witnessed.

I am Dyslexic. Recently I read that the British Government's GCHQ code-breakers have in the past and are currently employing people with Dyslexia to work on code-breaking and halting computer hacking. Apparently people with dyslexia have a powerful alternative thinking style and are able to recognize code patterns and omissions.

This book most likely seems an odd mix of subjects but the reasons it has been created this way is as follows. I had a list of correspondence that I had accumulated when I was a founder member and the first secretary to the British Parachute Association. I wanted to list it for the benefit of members but diaries are boring, so I have entered it in snippets. And then there are stories and poems that I wanted to share with you, some that I found amusing and others that created fear and some that will create thought and hopefully debate.

DYSLEXIA

Due to dyslexia I was unable to study very well from books. Also when people were present it made it almost impossible to study anything. As I also suffer from dyscalculia it takes me longer than the average person to remember figures, work out ways to calculate but I get there in the end.

I am thankful that I had fast physical reactions which saved me from many dangerous situations.

DYSCALCULIA

The affliction dyscalculia used to bring fear
as it means unable to calculate
My teachers smacked you around the ear
But now things are different, there are rules
Children are not forced to study by rote but
often end up being sent to special schools.

MUTATIONS

I think that it is a good job that people are born with mutations like dyslexia. If all humans were born with the same type of brain and then all of them were taught by rote.
Then we would all do the same thing, want the same thing and do the same things. Wouldn't that be boring. We would not have advanced and would still be behaving like monkeys; well I suppose a lot still do!
It is the difference in people that is always interesting.

In the summer of 2014; Professor M P. Gerkema PhD
encouraged me to finish writing a book called
Building The Khufu Pyramid-Shedding New Light.
At the time I wrote this poem.

DOUBLE DUTCH

Dutch Professor Menno Gerkema PhD
is studying the effect of circadian
time and light on you and me

His wife, the lovely Barbara Werner
helps him in studying time
or the effect of time, that's Zeitgeber

It is all to do with biological Anthropology
Primates and ancestors of the human species
I am afraid it is all 'double-dutch' to me

MY WORD

I found poetry when I found word
It corrects the spelling of every word
Being dyslexic was to me; a bind
WORD gave me; peace of mind
Writing gives me relaxation
and an inner satisfaction
I became literate, changed my world
I now communicate around the world

Note. Microsoft Word.

A WORD ABOUT WORD.

A word about word, a tool to command
Truly fantastic, particularly for a dyslexic
Corrects every word, sets right without demand

Written by Aesthete 2000 USA. allpoetry.com.

RELEASE, RELIEF, RENEWAL

You can release that inner turmoil
We all miss that turning, hit the rut
get on the wrong road, dark clouds appear
Write, open up, untie that knot in your gut

When a person writes, and creates
a story, poem, prose or ode
it will show a state of mind
a mood, modus vivendi, mode

We are all subject to moody moods
Fits of utter madness or despair
Doubts, regrets, remorse are with us all
Writing helps to sooth, and clear the air.

By Simpleton on Feb 18, 2010. © Bernard Green.

THERE ARE THREE SECTIONS TO THIS BOOK.

PART 1

Information on early parachuting in the UK, followed by the development of skydiving and the formation of THE BRITISH PARACHUTE ASSOCIATION.

PART 2

Autobiographical, stories about events that might be interesting to a variety of readers. And stories that are a mix of fact and fiction to create thought and discussion.

PART 3

Is an assortment of poems and stories. I like writing about people so there are lots of 'people poems'. Also there is a mix of others, Nature, Political and poems to make you think and perhaps debate.

WARNING. There is some adult suggestion within certain poems and stories that is only suitable for adults within Part 2 and 3 of this book

1946-49

My teachers hit me
Had not heard of Dyslexia
WORD helps me create

Senryu. 5-7-5 syllables. WORD is on Microsoft

MALAYSIA

When as a sailor, I landed in Penang
I loved this far Eastern City
Little did I realize that I would wed
a Chinese girl living in Kelang
My next port of call was Singapore
I watched the coolies working hard
Amused to see their hair-less legs
Then I met an attractive whore
"Call for a taxi, Mr Orang-puteh man"
As we walked along the promenade
She wanted a kiss, throwing back her head
I looked up her wide nostrils, and ran.
A food stall, it was ages since I ate
I felt at ease with these people
I had walked around the town alone
Ate nasi-goreng without sodium glutamate
Admired black haired girls wearing cheongsam
That showed the sinuous curves of slim figures
It did not occur to me that my future wife
might be in a pushchair or a pram
When I was serving in the British Army
She came to England as a nurse
In a restaurant, she walked past me
I was fixated to marry her, was I barmy?
It took a hard year and more
To get her to say "yes" to me
We have been married thirty-three years

I would like another score
She is my best friend and mate
She is like a mother hen
And I think she is rather rare
I'm pleased I asked her for a date
She is my cook, carer and advisor
We've had a few tantrums and tears
She has saved my life on two occasions
I could not wish for anyone wiser.

Note. My tantrums and tears did not last very long.
Orang-puteh man meant 'white person' in Malay.

A WOMAN I NEVER MET

The nicest woman that I never met
Teaching, coaxing me from over the sea
Three thousand miles separated me
from her and yet I felt her warmth
and enjoyed her intelligence
A mother, teacher, poet, potter and artist
A pal, a friend, a leader that is sadly missed.

Note. She was called Aesthete2000 and published on Allpoetry.com. It was Aesthete that encouraged me to write, bless her. I have placed some of her poems in my books I have also included some poems written by Anaisnais a lady poet that lives in Wales and also gave me excellent advice when I first started writing poetry.

DISAPPOINTMENT

Anticipation
queued all day to see the Queen
drove past at high speed.

Senryu. Note. My son was five years of age.

BEING STILL IS BORING

Still sunny days, hot boring burning sun
turning people to drink and drugs
Others engage in sport, adrenaline for some

There is no magic in a becalmed boat
the senses become dull, becalmed
Flowing movement keeps interest afloat

Sometimes it is nice to sit still
But being immobile makes you fat
and stiff, and can make you very ill

Motionless creatures have no interest for me
Movement always catches the observant eye
Like an albatross over the sea, a delight to see.

REMORSE

My teacher asked in the year of 1944
"Who made that affluvior, please tell
one of you has made an obnoxious smell"?
What a marvellous instrument, the brain
to hear a word once and forever retain
The girl beside me was dragged out the door!
For I had made that obnoxious odour

Note. The girl next to me got sorely wacked!
So no one heard a peep out of me.
I kept quiet in more ways than one.

PART 1

PARACHUTING

PARACHUTING, 1950's

PEACE OF MIND.

It was in the latter half of the 1950's that I started to parachute when I joined the parachute club at Fairoaks Aerodrome Nr Woking in Surrey. This club was sponsored by the GQ Parachute Company of Woking I did my first eight jumps there. My first jump was on the 9/7/1958, these were not static line jumps but free-fall, counting three seconds then pulling the ripcord. And that was from 1,500ft. It does not feel very high as you could see people's faces watching you from the ground. My parachuting certificate was No. 57 of 13/10/1960 and signed by Lord Brabazon.

There was a club room and a shed where the parachutes were packed. They had about six GQ parachutes supplied by GQ. They did not own an aircraft and hired an Auster four-seater aircraft or sometimes a Tiger Moth for those people that could jump without an instructor in attendance.

When jumping from the Tiger Moth as there were two separate cockpits the pilot sat in the back seat and the parachutist sat with one leg in the front cockpit and one leg outside and crouched forward to avoid the slipstream. It was exciting and better still when at the required height and with a wave the jumper asked the pilot to cut the throttle back; then you climbed out, closed the side hatch and secured it with a bolt. Then walked forward and peered over the front of the lower wing with the heat of the exhaust beating on your face in the blast of the propeller.

Having ascertained or thought that you were in the correct position to fall and float to the landing site you jumped off. In those days there was no knowledge of Skydiving, you just fell. After hooks on my boots got hooked up for a while in the rigging of a deploying chute I took up the habit of holding my toes in a Jack-knife diving position.

This was before sleeves came into use and the rigging deployed from the backpack, They were tightly pulled into webbing loops and made you rock side to side as they pulled out, on more than one occasion they did not come out of the loops and reserves were thrown so then we started attaching elastic bands to the webbing loops and the rigging was attached to them, any problem the elastic broke off.

The parachutes at that time were all circular white without any steering. All you could do is pull hard down on the harness risers to side-slip but it did not make a lot of difference to where you were heading. I only got eight jumps in my first year despite turning up every weekend. The reason being that too much time was spent with pencil and paper working out wind speed versus aircraft speed and ascertaining wind direction and waiting to hire aircraft.

Later when I went to the French Skydiving School at Chalon-Sur–Soane I learnt a valuable lesson. They owned their own aircraft and they just chucked a toilet roll out of the plane and watched where it landed to find the direction and distance. Also their parachutes were far better than the English ones. The harness was fully adjustable and comfortable and the chutes were steerable.

I had been informed in England that a parachute only malfunctioned once in 20.000 openings but I had two malfunctions in eight jumps during the first year of my time at Fairoaks. The first was when my parachute tried to turn inside out and ended up with three lines over the middle and it ended up looking like a big brassiere. It was spinning and when I threw the reserve it started to go into what I said looked like a Big Bra so I pulled it back and it wrapped around me like a mummy. I got a smashed Coccyx when I landed on the concrete hangar apron. It meant I could not sit down for a year. But I carried on jumping with a big rubber cushion sown into my jump-suit. It made me look as though I had a large posterior.

On 15th May 1959 I purchased a complete new rig from GQ parachute Company, Number 352206. It had a harness with a big circular release box, and backpack with an orange and white quartered 28ft circular canopy. The cost was about £300.0.0. This canopy was a new design for jet aircraft as it was designed to open slowly at high velocity. When it opened, it reminded me of the big curtains at the cinema slowly opening, it nearly caught me out once, I have written about that in the story 'Where's the body'.

The reserve chute was a completely new design being packed in something like a woman's handbag. When required to use it the parachutist pulled the handle which released the bag and threw it out to the side where it deployed and was in no danger of tangling with the main chute. I confidently wore this reserve for the next six jumps with the peace of mind of being over confident. Then I decided to repack it and to demonstrate the superiority of my latest acquisition I invited all of the club members to watch as I stood on the packing table to pull and throw my handbag. Please bear in mind I was not used to throwing handbags. I pulled and pulled and it would not come out its case, so I asked other males to try to pull it out! Nobody could budge it. It just would not work and yet on examination there was nothing that appeared to be wrong.

But the peace of mind was destroyed and I reverted to using the American 24ft surplus reserve with the rip-stop nylon canopy. I never had an emergency to use a reserve chute again. I put this down to the training I got in France, and being in a stable face to earth position when deploying the chute. Also I started using cotton sleeves to encase the main parachute, which I started to manufacture on my return from France.

The sleeves were the same length as the canopy with a flap turned back to stop the canopy coming out until the lines were completely deployed from the loops holding the lines over that flap, this slowed the opening. This ensured a smooth deployment and reduced the shock load when falling from high altitude and reaching terminal velocity. Prior to the use of sleeves we used to get covered in bruises from the harness and this caused me to have a Mastectomy due to a benign tumour.

I got a refund on the reserve, but perhaps I would not have got that refund if my main chute had failed in those ten jumps, that's an awful thought. In those early days at Fairoaks we were jumping from 1,500ft in unstable positions with three second delays which meant the chutes did not open quickly and cleanly. And there were only 10 seconds left before hitting the ground if you could not get the reserve deployed in the next 5 seconds. So I started travelling to other airfields where there were no height restrictions. This led to many adventures starting out with the peace of mind of being unaware of the problems that could and did occur.

THE BIG BRA

In the 1950's my friends and I were parachuting at Fairoaks Aerodrome near Woking. There was a big drawback here because there was a height restriction of 3,000ft due to being close to London Airport. We were not trained with static lines as is the case nowadays, but after being dispatched from an Auster Aircraft by Jim Basnett or Peter Lang we had 3 to 5seconds free-fall before pulling the ripcord.

On the subject of reserve chutes, the practice was to open the reserve that was in front of you and grab a hand-full of canopy and throw it out to the side and try and get it away from any failed canopy above you. If you did not succeed it would turn into a Roman-Candle (the parachute streams out into the other chute and they do not open) and you would die.

On the 21st of June 1959 at Fairoaks my canopy tried to turn inside out due to the slow opening and it looked like a huge brassiere as three lines were over the top. I threw the reserve, it went out and around me and then directly into one side of the big brassiere, I grabbed the nylon reserve canopy and feverishly pulled it back, I was now spinning and the material wrapped around me like an Egyptian Mummy, I could not see a thing. I just waited to hit the grass airfield. Then I heard a voice, it was not my guardian angel. It was a chap-called George Bottomley yelling fifty feet, forty- thirty. Georges name means; The Bottom field, but it did not help me because I hit the concrete apron outside the hangars. I was in the Rowley Bristow hospital for two days.

The pain was terrible, I had crushed my Coccyx. If you do not know what that is, it is the remnant of our tail at the bottom of the spine. I could not sit on my bum, for about two years, I sat on my thigh. At the cinema I had to sit perched on the seat in the up position, much to the annoyance of anyone seated behind me.

BIG BUM

I started parachuting again on the 31st of June and won a competition at Fairoaks, if you see any photos of me it looks like I have a big bum but I had a rubber cushion sewn into my orange coloured overalls. Orange? Yes. Was I not rather daring when everyone else had grey or white jump suits, and I also painted my helmet to make it look like the spotted lady-bird.

I had purchased a brand new type of GQ reserve parachute that when you pulled the handle it came out like a handbag, which you could then throw out away from the failed chute. So now I had a handbag as well as an orange jumpsuit and a Lady-bird helmet. Don't get ideas about me.

In two separate parachuting incidents I fractured my coccyx and my spine in three places yet I am still able to touch my toes so I am extremely lucky. The unusual reason is that through being bloody-minded I never had any plaster cast or treatment apart from physiotherapy which meant I kept my muscles. The specialist had told me 'If I put you in plaster you will lose your muscles and it is your muscles that keep you standing, not your bones.'

I visited Ginger Green in Stoke Mandeville Spine injury

ward when he became paralysed due to a bad landing. There were sixteen men in the ward and I asked each about his accident. One had been run over by a military hover-craft he would have been OK but the captain shut off the engine and the hover-craft settled down on him. The other one dived off Southend pier in the morning and then dived off in the afternoon, but the tide had gone out. The other twelve fell off of ladders. Life is fragile aint it.

SITTING IN AN OAK TREE

On the 11TH January 1959 on my eleventh jump at Fairoaks Aerodrome I was despatched at the wrong place and with a circular 28ft plain chute. I could not avoid landing in a large oak tree right on the edge of the road so I crossed my legs as I plunged through the branches and then luckily the chute tangled and I bounced to a very prickly stop. But it was very uncomfortable as I was sitting on a barbed wire fence and every movement really hurt my bum, so I sat very still and waited for the club members to find me.

A lady drove past then stopped and reversed back, she sat in the car looking at me. I just looked back thinking she was going to get out of the car. She then drove off at high speed. The club members rescued me but the club chute was ruined. We did not get a chance to look at it as the Police arrived having been told that there was a dead parachutist in an oak tree, lucky me.

MY TIME LINE, PARACHUTING

15th Jan 1960 I obtained my Instructors Licence at Stapleford Tawney. The examiners were Mike Reilly and Peter Lang.

18th Sept 1960. IRISH PARACHUTING RALLY AT WESTON AERODROME, LUCAN.

Visiting parachutists Mike Reilly, James McLoughlin. Peter Lang. Stan Anstee. Dennis Smith. UK. Charles Stewart, AUS. William Sparke, AUS. George Blanchard, NZ. and myself.

I jumped from an Avro Cadet EI-ALP. From 6,600 ft. Pilot B. Miller, This jump (My 64th) is in the story of the 'Black Hole' in my book Dunce or Dyslexic. The second was from a Tiger Moth EI-AHA from 2,200 ft. Pilot Capt. P.W.Kennedy.

The story about the first jump and the Black Hole was about something that is known as Pilot Fixation and was named after some pilots in WW2 shooting up trains actually flew into them. On this jump I was right over the black hole of a factory chimney. I got a fixation on it and thought wouldn't it be interesting to go down inside the chimney! I had to mentally chastise myself to open my chute.

25th Sept 1960. My first jump with a canopy sleeve that I had manufactured. This was at Shoreham Airfield, Sussex from 4,400ft. Very smooth opening; what a difference from coming abruptly to a stop from 120mph. My log book comment was. No shocks no bruising, wonderful.

13th Oct 1960 I RECEIVED MY FAI PARACHUTE CERTIFICATE A and B No 57 Signed by Lord Brabazon. Cert A = 10 jumps. Cert B= 25 Free-fall jumps, including 15 over 10 seconds, 5 of 20 sec's, one of 30sec's with ability to hold heading and stop a spin.

16th Oct 1960. I Modified my GQ. 20ft Orange and white quartered, circular parachute by cutting out panels with a razorblade.
The first jump after this modification was a night drop. I noted that I was very pleased with the result.

B.P.A. TIME LINE, 22nd Oct 1960 FORMATION OF THE BRITISH PARACHUTE ASSOCIATION.

I met in a London coffee bar with friends on the 22nd Oct 1960 to consider the formation of a Parachute association. GH Hoeschle (Herb) President of The Parachute Club of Canada was there to give advice, he and his wife were on holiday in the UK. Mike Reilly proposed setting up The British Parachute Association. It was agreed that he was to be Chairman, Stanley Anstey was responsible for the accounts, I was the Hon, Secretary. My wife Ann was there to take notes. Now it is a highly organised association responsible for the safe operation of Parachuting and Skydiving in this country. There is a photograph of this momentous meeting taken in the coffee bar in my first book called 'Dunce or Dyslexic. I used the pseudonym Simpleton for that book.

I used my house 'Wilmslow' in Runfold, Near Farnham, Surrey as the B.P.A. Office, and then followed by using my British Skydiving office at The Toll House, Runfold. As I am Dyslexic it is quite interesting how I managed to be Secretary of the BPA, quite simply I had a secretary for my Café business and British Skydiving that I used to dictate the letters to. This young lady was Pamela Manley who married my father and gave me a delightful sister called Amber. I wrote a poem which is one of my favourites called 'Ambers Oak'.

YOUTH

Oh, brash youth
I envy your ignorance
Unaware of serious pain
Loss of loved one
or mental anguish

MORNING THOUGHTS

I did go to school
But I can't spell or calculate
I am dyslexic
Senryu.

I'm still yearning and learning.

SAFE ADRENALINE RUSH

I think it will be very soon
you need not take a rocket to the moon
You will be able to walk the Grand Canyon
and enjoy the scenery with a companion

With 3D goggles and computer technology
Walking on a treadmill imitating its geology
There will be no need to go on holiday
Just don the gear and play Technology

This can create a holiday for me and you
Using Google 360 degree camera street view
Just put on the headsets and Google goggles
and sky-dive while a wind tunnel pummels.

INTERNET

When dating take care
That sweet looking face might hide
a devil, tread with care

Senryu, 5-7-5 syllables

AUTHOR

Authors work consumes
excitement leaps from pages
exhilaration.

A Senryu poem by Aesthete2000

WHERE'S THE BODY (SKYDIVING)

I did sigh well after I did a parachute jump at Sywell Aerodrome, Near Northampton in the UK during the 1960s. I had been parachuting and skydiving for two years when Pat Slattery and I decided to go to Sywell to jump. We enjoyed going to different aerodromes for a number of reasons. The travelling, jumping from different aircraft and most of all I enjoyed looking at the scenery as I fell through the sky. Only it did not feel like falling until this particular day. It feels like floating on a soft cushion. It's like you are lying on a cushion of air. The countryside below looks like a huge fruit bowl below you from 6,000ft up. The fruit bowl below with its hedges, Copses and different coloured small fields never failed to amaze me. There is nothing like England for shades of green. As you free-fall it appears that you are descending into and below the rim of that bowl, if you are not carrying an altimeter this means you should be getting ready to open your chute. The only time you get a sensation of your speed is when you pass down the side of a cloud. I remember when I first passed through a cumulus cloud and flinched because it looked hard but you do not feel it. All you get is moisture collecting on your face.

This day I would experience speed and fear. Sywell aerodrome was a vast expanse of grass but it is not flat. When you view from the Control Tower area the land rises, it is not a hill but just a bump in the terrain. There was no reason to alter our altimeters as we would open our chutes above 1,500ft. It was a cloudless summer day, the aircraft was a Cessna.
We each wanted to spot for ourselves, that is direct the pilot to the exit point which we estimated would allow our drifting to land where we would not have to walk a long way to get a cup of tea.

I left the plane at 7,OOO ft. I had previously been using a standard 28ft GQ parachute and this was before the use of sleeves which enclosed the canopy to reduce the opening shock. The opening shock of an un-sleeved parachute at terminal velocity (over 120mph) kept bruising my body and if I wore a string vest it looked as if I had a fishnet tattoo. The large harness buckle on the British chutes bruised my chest so often I had to have a Mastectomy operation. No not a vasectomy, yes I know women have Mastectomies. I felt and looked as though Shylock had taken his pound of flesh.

This day I was using my brand new orange and white quartered parachute purchased from The GQ Parachute Company. The attraction of this chute was that it had

23

been designed for pilot ejection from high speed aircraft. Jet planes were getting faster and Jet pilots parachutes were being blown to shreds by the opening shock. This chute was designed to open slowly. It would stream out and remain in what was often described as a candle shape. '

So often with early pioneers chutes they streamed out and never opened and as they were white it was described as a candle. This new design would remain in a candle effect until the drag caused a reduction in speed then it would open slowly at first then snap open. It was smooth and graceful as opposed to the brutal shocks that I had previously experienced, with an old army style chute. On one occasion it caused one of my boots to come off, I never found it.

I really enjoyed this free-fall, trying out aerobatic manoeuvres, viewing the countryside, feeling the rush of warm air pummelling my cheeks. I looked at my altimeter. I had got carried away and had gone below 2,000ft. On reaching for my ripcord, which should have been in an elasticated pocket on the left of my chest. I could not feel it. I looked for it, was not there.

I had ten seconds to live. I turned my attention to operate the reserve chute clipped to the harness on front of my chest. This was a 24ft parachute that I had to open and throw into the slipstream. As my hands closed over the reserve it caused me to roll over onto my back and that made the main ripcord to come floating over my shoulder from where it had been hiding! Ah, I thought I would rather descend on the main chute and grabbed the ripcord and pulled. As the parachute streamed out I thought, 'Oh No! That was a big mistake'. I had wasted three second's. Now I had 7seconds or less to live. But I had not been counting; I probably had about 3 seconds to live.

Most accidents are not caused by a single action or inaction. They are usually caused by a combination of events. I had seen a parachutist's death caused by him getting too engrossed in aerobatic activities, then getting too low. Then his rather large gloves which helped in skydiving manoeuvres impeded him opening the reserve chute.

One weekend when I was parachuting at Kidlington Aerodrome I had seen a very experienced Army Officer getting his exit point wrong and heading to land in a built up area. He then chose a nice lawn to land on but his feet caught on an unseen phone wire which tipped him over to cause him to land on his head. He died in hospital.

Now feeling secure that my chute was going to open I looked down. At that split second; all I could see was part of a hedge, a grass verge and the edge of a road. I could even see the blades of grass! There was no time for thought. My whole body cramped up and I retched violently at the same moment.

Then a strange sense of peace and quiet came over me and I thought I was in heaven. I opened my eyes and found I was standing upright on the grass verge outside the airfield hedge, I am not dead. I had landed on my feet and did not even fall over. I unclipped the harness and stood beside the empty road, I took off my helmet and overalls and threw them on the grass, the sun was hot and life felt wonderful.

I considered what had happened, the final opening of

the chute had caused a bounce by the stretching of the nylon suspension cords, it was at that precise point my feet touched the ground without any impact. I did have a guardian angel. Pat was unaware of what had happened for he was floating down to the airfield.

A 7cwt white van came hurtling up the road and stopped beside me, the driver jumped out and walked past me. He looked around at the scene of discarded parachutes and helmet then turned to me and said "Where's the body"? "What body," I asked; obviously my euphoria had stopped me thinking. "The body of the parachutist, his chute did not open". "That is me" I replied. He looked at me in a very strange way, then without a word got in the van and drove away. He must have thought I was Mr Cool, but I think I was in shock.

I was on the opposite side of a field from the control tower. I think this narrow road led to Sywell Grange which is north of the Airfield. Apparently I had disappeared behind the rising ground as or before the chute opened. Eventually Pat came and collected me. This event did not put me off as I continued to Skydive and opened the first skydiving school in the UK at Thruxton, Aerodrome Near Andover, Hampshire.

I do have the feeling that I am alive today because before I started parachuting I read all the books on the subject including all the guys that experimented with fixed wings, most of those guys died in entanglements.
The moment any panic sets in you are lost.

BRITISH SKYDIVING CLUB.

SKYDIVING IN STYLE.

RAF Mildenhall in Suffolk, England, was the base of 7513th Tactical Group of the United States Air Forces in Europe. Unfortunately my parachuting log book for the period was lost in a flood but it was in the 1960s that I received a telephone call at the office of British Skydiving Ltd at The Toll House, Runfold, Farnham in Surrey. It was an Officer of the USAF at Mildenhall and he asked if I could supply two Skydivers for the next Air Show at the base which was only a couple of weeks away. I said yes and he asked where the nearest airfield to my residence was, I told him Fairoaks Aerodrome, Nr Woking, Surrey. He said he would send an aircraft to collect us on the day before the show.

A member of my sky-diving club, Sherdy Vatsndal agreed to come with me and on the Saturday afternoon we arrived at Fairoaks to find a beautiful Military Beaver Aircraft waiting for us. We even got a salute from the pilot. Without any consultations we were whisked away and after a wonderful flight skirting around the North of London we landed at Mildenhall where a Staff car was waiting for us at the side of the peri-track. We were driven to the Officers' quarters. I noticed that the car engine was running while we disembarked from the beaver and the driver left the engine running at all times. When I asked him why he said that he was instructed to leave it running as starting the engine caused more wear than when it was running continuously. I thought this rather odd. It might apply in sub-zero climates but I thought it a waste of petrol.

We dined in the Officers Mess and were amazed at the choice of food available and the huge portions which meant the plates were twice the size of the dinner plates that I used in my café. We went to bed early and again at breakfast there was a stunning array of food.

I was surprised at the mixture and quantity being consumed of juices, cereals, steaks with two eggs sunny side up on top, followed by pancakes. No wonder those guys were all very large.

I had always been brought up to eat everything on my plate and still do, even when the food is free and self-service I never put more than I can eat on my plate. Perhaps it is due to being a child in the 2nd world war does that. Nearly all the Americans in the self-service restaurant had steaks that they took two bites from and just dipped into the yolks of their two eggs. The amount of food left on the plates astonished me.

We all assembled in the briefing room. At the British Air-shows someone would say to the Skydivers something like this. "After the Stampe aircraft has finished his aerobatics you drop in on your chutes, OK, chaps." Here we listened to a programme run second by second with talk of the jet fighters starting their approach run from Swansea in Wales passing over the airfield at Mach 1.

It was not very comforting to hear that we were to jump from 12,000 ft. as those fighters were approaching at the speed of sound. After we were asked how long we would be in free-fall and how long under the canopy we would be, we were given a time to exit the Beaver aircraft at a number of minutes and seconds past the hour. Then the briefing officer said, "The time is," and everybody held up their left arms and adjusted their chronometers. I never owned a watch, I still do not wear one as for some reason I cannot stand having anything on my wrist. But I held my arm up to be in with the crowd, Sherdy also held up his arm as he had a watch but it did not have a second hand on it!

The next hours are a blur but now we are at 12,000ft in the Beaver aircraft cruising round in a circle waiting for the time to drop which we had agreed with the pilot to give us the signal to go. It was so pleasant lying on the floor with our heads out the doorway watching the air-show from above. The airfield was covered with helicopters all buzzing around at a low altitude playing some sort of war game when the pilot shouted "GO" I thought, Bloody hell this is dangerous, I am going to get minced up by those helicopter blades. But the brain works at enormous speed in these situations and I debated the issues like this. I have got to go now as there are two fighter jets coming here at Mach1. I do not wish to meet them in the air. I will jump and if those helicopters are still below me I will open slightly higher and drift off to the side of the airfield.

I jumped and Sherdy followed. I must say I did not look at the view as my eyes were glued on those helicopters and my brain was saying mincemeat-mincemeat. After falling for 30seconds and we were about 6,000ft the helicopters dispersed to the corners of the field. Now that was organization, at the British shows it might be 10 minutes between events. Now perfectly relaxed we landed, but as our chutes slowly collapsed to the ground there was an almighty Ka-boom, Ka-Boom as the two fighter jets broke the speed of sound over the airfield and we watched their blazing red-blue exhausts disappear over the countryside at about 500ft above the ground.

Could those pilots see us as they approached? I doubt that we would have shown on their radar at all as even Hot-air balloons with their propane tanks do not show up very well.

We were then again whisked away by car to the restaurant for a coffee, tea or Coca Cola and choice from piles of pies, pasties apple pies and pastries or donut, muffin, cake, Cheesecake, fruit pie with ice cream or custard. I was in the English Air force for a month before I got chucked out because I was dyslexic, also I was in the British Army for three years and I never ever saw food like that except the Regiments Boxers got steaks for some reason. After our tea and cake, Notice the singular (cake) we were driven to the Beaver Aircraft and flown back to Fairoaks before it got dark. This was truly an adventure into the unknown and an interesting look into how the other side live. Americans are not just English speaking people that live over the water they are completely different in many ways.

DEADLY COMBINATIONS. Part A

THE WAR LOVER.

The film THE WAR LOVER was about a World War 2 B17 Flying Fortress pilot played by the actor Steve McQueen as Captain Buzz Rickman with the co-pilot played by Robert Wagner and the ball turret gunner by Michael Crawford. The film is based on a novel by John Hersey.

It required two scenes where the crew bale out over the English Channel. British Skydiving Ltd was contracted by British Columbia Pictures to provide the parachutists and the parachutes. The team was selected from the members of the British Skydiving Club which operated at Thruxton aerodrome near Andover Hampshire. All were very experienced Skydivers and members of the British Parachute Association. It was so pleasant to have Peter Lang along with us as he was the man that despatched me on my very first parachute jump which was at Fairoaks aerodrome which was a 3seconds freefall from 1,500ft. It was also such a great pleasure to have my mentor Mike Reilly with us. He was studying at the London School of Economics.

This part of the film is where the aircraft is returning to England across the English Channel from a bombing mission and is losing height due to being hit by anti-aircraft gun-fire. The bomb doors are open as there was a bomb that had failed to release.

On the 9th of January we all did three jumps in four hours, from the B17 on to Manston Airfield in Kent including repacking the seat types we were using for the film. Tony Miller threw his reserve when he could not find the ripcord to the seat type. Dennis Smith got concussion.

The full story about the death of Mike Reilly is in my book Dunce or Dyslexic. It mystified me how a strong athletic water polo player like Mike Reilly could have drowned this way. Since then I have read of many airmen and soldiers that have drowned when wearing a parachute harness that did not have a release mechanism for the canopy. At the British Skydiving Club we all had the American harnesses that had the Capewell quick release system.

31

One of the things I did not write about was those seat types. They were WW2 manufacture Sutton seat types that had the large harness central locking box and the leg straps had to be looped around the body harness. It did not matter how much you tightened the harness, leaving yourself in the most uncomfortable crouching position. When the chute deployed you could feel the harness moving around your body making you feel that you were going to fall out of the harness. When the chute was fully deployed the shoulder buckles were above our heads.

I jumped out of the port side gunners door and on the second jump did not dive hard enough which meant that the slipstream rolled me along the fuselage narrowly missing the tail. If I had hit my head on the tail it would have probably rendered me unconscious and I would not have been able to operate my chute.

It was such a difference from skydiving, first tumbling caused by the turbulence from the aircraft and the large parachute bundle on your bum (posterior) then after at least five seconds free-falling to ensure enough speed to pull the chute out of the pack. Pull the ripcord unless you have lost it (which happens as it gets tucked under the bulky military clothing) the chute then streams away with the cords pulling out of the elastic bands that we attached to the pockets rather than use the webbing loop pockets. This was because during my membership of the parachute club at Fairoaks Aerodrome I had seen the parachute cords jam in those webbing loops and fail to deploy the main chute more than twice.

After doing an aerial rumba caused by the parachute cords coming detached from the elastics the parachute bangs violently open (sense of joy) and the harness then seems as though it is going to unravel which was a horrible feeling, then there was no steering and a very hard landing as it was a plain 24ft canopy.

There were two B17's at Manston but we only used one. They seemed to use the other one for spares. John Crewdson the pilot flew stunts for many other films including James Bond films. He died on the 26th June 1983 while flying a helicopter during the making of a film.

It is now possible to purchase a DVD of this film I obtained my copy on the 23rd March 2015. Having now seen the film I see that there was a wardrobe error in the cockpit scene as Steve McQueen and Robert Wagner are wearing parachutes with a parachute canopy quick release system which was not patented until Aug/11/1954 by Rocket Engineering Corp No 2870509 the inventor being John A. Gaylord. This was known as The Capewell Release system and ideal to have if descending into water or in high winds.

20th June 1961 patent number #2,802,252. It was originally called the Gaylord Release and used by the US Navy. We were using the British Seat type with a twenty four foot white canopy and a Sutton harness. This harness was made of white cotton and was used by British and American crews in World War 11. American parachutes during 1943 to 1945 had white 24ft canopies. The pilots had harness type A4 QAC (Quick Attachable Chest). This harness also had the large quick release box which sat centrally on the chest and was for fitting a 24ft chest pack parachute very quickly.

Had Mike been wearing a harness with Capewell release system I have no doubt he would have survived. I have also seen a statement on the web that Mike fell to his death. In the film you can see that he descends safely into the water on the white chute and he lands right in front of the Motor Torpedo Boat.

Note. The boat crew having caught his chute the boat engine was stopped. Then a gust of wind tore the chute out of their hands and blew him away across the sea. By the time the engine was re-started and they caught up with him, he had drowned. As the parachute towed him across the water a bow wave was created by the water flowing over his head and shoulders.

The trouble was that first of all the crew had to start a small engine called a 'Donkey Engine' which was then used to start the huge diesel engine. It took too long.

PARACHUTING & SKYDIVING.

When there is an accident, there are usually a number of reasons as to why it occurred. One reason might turn out to be an incident that the participant can discuss later in the club or pub.

But when other elements occur the combination can cause serious injury or be fatal. My first example is about "Ginger," who was a friend of mine from Fleet in Hampshire. He started parachuting at the British Skydiving Club, at Thruxton in the early 1960s. He was a painter-decorator by trade and was fit, muscular and of medium build. He progressed to Free-fall and was a competent and safe skydiver.

He met a lady and then did not attend the club for a few months. One day he arrived and introduced the lady that he had just married. He told me that he wished to demonstrate to her his prowess in the sport. I had no worries about his ability, it was a fine day with a light wind, and the students were already jumping from the club De-Havilland Rapide aircraft.

The airfield was a huge grass expanse with a tarmac runway and a tarmac track around the perimeter. Ginger's parachute was an American C9 28ft circular chute with a double L cut-out for turning and forward drive. There were no apparent problems. He drifted down and landed on the runway. But for some reason he broke his spine and was never able to walk again. I was very impressed by the loyalty and care that Gingers wife gave to him.

SUMMARY

When I was talking to Ginger later at Stoke Mandeville spinal hospital he told me that during the week before the accident he had fallen off a ladder and injured one of his knees. He most probably would not have made this parachute jump under normal circumstances but he wanted to demonstrate his prowess to his wife. As he came in to land and unable to avoid the hard runway he thought about his injured knee and decided to land on one leg. This action caused his spine to twist and break on the impact.

Here we have five apparently unconnected reasons for this tragedy.

First. There was the knee injury.

Second. There was a gap in training and the instructors were unaware of the knee injury.

Third. His desire to demonstrate his ability to his wife overcame caution.

Fourth. His decision to favour one leg on landing.

Fifth. Unfortunately landing on the hard tarmac runway. He might have got away with it on the grass or the ploughed ground around the edge of the airfield.

SKYDIVING AT BIGGIN HILL.

It was the 1960s that that I ended up covered in household rubbish at The Biggin Hill Air show at Bromley in Kent. I was invited to provide a display at the air show which was a prestigious event. I also took the British Skydiving Ltd display caravan in which the public could examine the equipment we used and obtain information on the courses available and the cost.

Our team consisted of myself and two members of the British Skydiving Club; one was Pat Slattery I regret that I cannot remember the other chap's names. In our club we had a skydiver and pilot named Kenneth Vos. I had arranged with him to supply an aircraft and be pilot for us.

The atmosphere at Biggin Hill was extremely exciting for we had never jumped or flown here before. It had been an important RAF airfield during the Battle of Britain and I wanted to view it from above. It is on a hill and surrounded by housing.

We had no idea what aircraft Ken would bring but we assumed it would be some-thing like a Cessna but at the last minute he flew in with an aeroplane none us had seen before, it was a Lancashire Aircraft EP9 Prospector. It was designed by Edgar Percival in the 1950s with a STOL performance which meant that it could take off and land in a short distance. I think this one had a "95 Lycoming engine with a maximum speed of 146mph and a rate of climb of 1,120ft/min (5.7m/s)

I believe that Ken was thinking of purchasing one of these to operate in Australia. They were designed with large detachable clamshell doors on the rear cargo hold and could be used for crop spraying, transporting wool bales or 45 Gallon drums of oil or fuel. The floor was sheet corrugated aluminium. There were only 27 of them built and there is one on display at the Museum of Army Flying at Middle Wallop in Hampshire England.

As I said Ken was late arriving so we had no time to examine our new jump-ship, it was time to go so we clambered into the hold at the back of this plane which I thought looked like a duck. Ken, the pilot was sitting high above our heads; I could only see his head and shoulders. With the engine noise he could not hear us even when we shouted. Ken knew the score as he was an experienced Skydiver so we were not too bothered about getting to the exit point in the sky so we would drift back onto the airfield. We sat on the aluminium floor as we taxied onto the runway; there were no seats, no straps or hooks on the floor.

We were rolling quite fast down the runway now, with the back doors off it was like the open back doors of a Hercules aircraft. It was an open gap of nearly 5ft wide. We were used to steady slow rate of climb take offs in Cessna's and De-Haviland Rapide's but suddenly Ken threw the nose of the plane up and started what seemed like an almost vertical climb, and we all started sliding on the smooth floor towards the open doorway. The parachutes would be useless as there was not enough height to operate them. I could find nothing to hold onto on the sides of the hold or the floor.

My fingernails dug into the grooves of the aluminium and found purchase on the heads of the rivets that held the floor in place. How the other two managed to hold on I just don't know. Ken now levelled out whether he heard us screaming I do not know, because after we jumped he returned to another airfield and I never saw him again.

We got to a jump height of about 6,000ft and started the run in, I could see we were off track and Ken could not hear our directions so I tried tapping his left shoulder to get him to veer to the left but there was no response so I punched his left shoulder very hard. Perhaps it annoyed him as we never got the aircraft to the exit point and now it was time to go, so out we jumped as we were not going to miss this opportunity to parachute down to Biggin Hill.

In free-fall I tracked like a swallow to get across the sky but when I opened my chute I knew I was doomed to land in the housing estate to the west of the field. As I have said the airfield is on a hill and now I could see a deep valley on the west side which was being filled with house hold garbage by the council. After considering my options I decided to land in the rubbish instead of a roof, electric wires or road. I hit the top of the heap and tumbled head over heels down the rubbish to the bottom of the heap. I was covered in crap but happy to be alive, we could have all very easily slid out that cargo hold. I clambered up to the top of the smelly rubbish and rolled the chute up in a bundle and caught a bus back to the main entrance of the airfield. I was happy to be smelly and not dead.

Nobody had inquired if we were safe when we went missing which is a bit strange. The other two guys managed to land safely on the west side of the airfield. We immediately got busy signing up new recruits in our Caravan for the rest of the day. I never saw Ken Vos again but I understood that he immigrated to Australia and did crop spraying out there.

You might like to know that the Insurance in case we landed on someone or damaged something was two shillings and six pence.

The old British Pounds Shillings and Pence, £.s.d. dating from the year 1066 until the 26th February 1971 was divided into eight Half Crowns, twenty Shillings and 240 pence. 2/6 was Half a Crown and worth 1/8th of One Pound or 30 pence. Half a Shilling was six pence. There were 480 Half pennies and 960 farthings to the pound.

BRITISH PARACHUTE ASSOCIATION, B.P.A. TIME LINE.

There are numerous letters from The Royal Aero club forwarded to my residence at "Wilmslow" Runfold to answer as secretary of the B.P.A. dated 23/Nov/1960 to 24/April/1961. It is unfortunate that many letters were lost due to a flood. Here is a sample of them.

23/NOV/1960 Letter from Sqn Ldr, Marks R.A.F. Headquarters Transport Command Royal Air Force, Upavon. Pewsey, Wiltshire.

Ref TC/48230/1/CA. Sqn Ldr Marks originally wrote to the Royal Aero Club but was informed by a Mrs Tomlinson to write to B.Green at Wilmslow.

On the 29/Nov/1960 I wrote to Mrs Tomlinson of the Royal Aero Club, asking her to invite Sqn, Ldr Marks to the next British Parachute Committee Meeting. He did attend.
Note. Mrs Tomlinson was secretary to the Aviation Secretary.

24/APR/1961 letter from E.A.J. Gardener Esq Officers mess 3rd Battalion the Parachute regiment, Guillemont barracks, Cove.

1/MAY/1961. My Letter to the treasurer Stan Anstee, where I enclose B.P.A. membership fees of 10/6 each for. Peter Hearn. John Thirtle, Alf Card, S, Phipps and D, Francombe.

6/MAY/1961.
BRITISH PARACHUTE ASSOCIATION AND
ROYAL AERO CLUB PANEL LIST

OF PARACHUTING EXAMINERS.
MIKE B REILLY, PETER LANG, JIM T BASNETT.

13/SEPT/1961.Letter from Handley Page Ltd to Bernard Green, British Parachute Association, Wilmslow, Runfold, Nr Farnham, Surrey.

13/SEPT/1961.Letter from Sun Life Insurance Co 3/6 Chancery Lane London WC2. Wanting to know about parachute clubs and if they have insurance cover?

14/SEPT/1961.Letter from Major Critchley, Bw. Brigade Major 152 9HO INF BDE Cameron Barracks Inverness. Inquiring about parachute clubs and instructors.

15/SEPT/1961.Letter from the Daily Telegraph to B. Green, Esq, Secretary , B.P.A..
This was in regard to parachuting photographs which I supplied for the Farnborough Air Show.
All of which disappeared.

21/SEPT/1961. Letter from Squadron Ldr T. Lockwood R.A.F. Liaison Officer RAF, Wethersfield, Nr Braintree Essex.
Requesting information about Parachuting in the UK.

21/SEPT 1961. Letter from Squadron Ldr T. Lockwood R.A.F. Liaison Officer RAF, Wethersfield, Nr Braintree Essex. Requesting information about Parachuting in the UK.

23/SEPT/1961. Letter from H.M.S Collingwood requesting information on clubs.

28/SEPT/1961. Letter sent to D, Corney about his B.P.A. membership fee of Ten shillings and six pence. Also information about the Oxford Parachute Club.

2/OCT/1961. I replied to a letter from Guy Voyce of 255, 49th ST NEW YORK, 17.N.Y. USA. He was asking for information on the British Parachute Championships.

4/OCT/1961. A letter sent to Mr Acheson explaining about clubs and costs. Also explained that subscriptions to the B.P.A. must be sent to Stanley Anstee, 37 Lambourne House Silwood Estate, London SE 16.

4/OCT/1961 Letter from Wren Codd 118408 Rodney Division Burgfield, Reading, Berks. Asking for list of clubs.

05/OCT/1961 Letter from Lt Harry M. Edwards USAF Personnel Services Officer 20th Air Base Squadron. United States Air Force APO 120, US Forces UK. Requesting information on Parachute clubs.

13/OCT/1961 letter from the safety equipment officer Westland Aircraft Yeovil. I advised him to contact Brian Porter of Graham St Swindon. Wilts as he operates at Staverton Airport.

21/NOV/1961. A letter from Lt Graham Wigan of the Green Jackets Brigade. Winchester. He had taken over the running of the Green Jackets Parachute Club. I answered his many queries.

3/DEC/1961. Air Navigation order exemption allowing B.Green, Mike Reilly and Stan Anstee to Parachute into Blackbushe Airport. Signed by Group Captain Caster.

This turned out to be very interesting as on the day

there was a weather front closing in. We took off in the centre of the weather front and jumped as the airport flag showed nil wind. We fell for thousands of feet down the side of the massive grey cloud which looked just like a solid cliff. For one crazy second I flinched as I thought I was going to hit it. It was exciting and allows me to understand the excitement for guys that jump off the mountain cliffs and fly 'The Wings'.

18/SEPT/1960 IRISH PARACHUTING RALLY AT WESTON AERODROME, LUCAN.

Visiting parachutists, Mike Reilly, James McLoughlin. Peter Lang. Stan Anstee. Dennis Smith. UK. Charles Stewart, AUS. William Sparke, AUS. George Blanchard, NZ.
I attended and jumped from an Avro Cadet EI-ALP. From 6,600 ft. Pilot B. Miller, and then a Tiger Moth EI-AHA from 2,200 ft. Pilot Capt. P.W.Kennedy.

The first jump (My 64th) is in the story of the Black Hole in my book Dunce or Dyslexic this is when I became fixated on a factory chimney.

SUCCESS

Don't judge success by the friends you have,
But by the enemies you've made.

THE BRITISH PARACHUTE CHAMPIONSHIPS.

6-7th/ MAY/ 1961
At Stapleford Tawney in Essex.
The wind speed 20/25 kts. I did two jumps,
One from 3000ft and the second from 5000ft.

Note. The competition was continued at Kidlington Aerodrome, Oxford on the 13/14th May using a Tripacer aircraft.

THE BRITISH OPEN PARACHUTE CHAMPIONSHIPS. SENIOR EVENT, COMPETITORS

(BEST THREE DISTANCES TO COUNT)

DENNIS SMITH:	Wanderers Club
CYRIL LANDAU:	Wanderers Club
FRED GAYLER:	British Parachute Club
PAULINE ADY	British Parachute Club
JOHN ROWE:	British Parachute Club
MIKE BROWSINSKI:	British Parachute Club
KEITH TEESDALE	Oxford Parachute Club
BERNARD GREEN	British Skydiving Club

I did two descents at Kidlington from 5.000 ft.

WORLD RECORDS 1959-60

Event No. I Jump from 3,000 ft. with a maximum delay of 10 seconds.
JOSEPH HINDICKY [Czechoslovakia], aggregate 'landing distance from centre of target in two jumps =1.02 metres (7th June, 1959).

Event No.2 Jump from 5,000 ft. with any delay between 15 and 20 seconds.

JAROSLAV JEHLlCKA (Czechoslovakia)) aggregate distance on two jumps = 0.445 metre (27th May, 1960).

ABILITY

A female can catch fish
as well as a fisherman
A King can catch crabs
as well as a commoner.

CHAIRS

Chairs must get stronger
Lawyers are waiting for their break
from those big wobbly bottoms

Haiku 5-7-5 Syllables.

FALLING OUT OVER SHOES (SKYDIVING)

It was on the 8th May 1961 that Mike Reilly, Martin Griffiths and myself travelled to Sywell Aerodrome in Northamptonshire in order to Skydive. I say Skydive as opposed to Parachuting because to parachute is a term used if you operate the parachute in order to leave an aircraft and arrive safely on the ground. Skydiving means there is the added attraction of doing aerobatic movements without the fear of landing badly on the

Gymnasium mat, or doing a belly flop in the water as the result of a bad dive.

To Skydive means flying as high as you can and delaying the opening of the parachute to enjoy the wonderful feeling of falling or even the sensation of flying when placing your body into a delta wing shape and seeing the ground pass underneath you. These days fabric wings are being used which extends the flying time considerably, they are being nicknamed the flying squirrels. My emblem for the British Skydiving Club was a flying squirrel. It is an unfortunate fact that most of the early pioneers that used wings of cloth or solid wings died while trying out their wings.

On arrival at Sywell Aerodrome we hired a Cessna 170. This aircraft had a single-engine, a metal fuselage with high fabric wings that were supported by a "V" strut that attached forward and level with the door. It was a four-seater but we removed the two rear seats and the door on the port side. We asked the pilot to fly as high as he could in one hour. This Aircraft was produced between 1948 to 1956 and the climb rate was supposed to be 690ft per minute, with a cruise speed of 121mph and a ceiling of 15,500ft. We would not be going above 12,000ft because there is always a danger of blackouts from lack of oxygen.

The sky was clear but there was a chill in the air, we had the RAF thin flying suits on over our normal clothes. We sat on the bare aluminium floor behind the pilot, Mike got in first, I think he knew it was going to be draughty, I sat in the middle and Martin sat at the door to do the spotting and direct the plot to the required exit point over the airfield.

I felt quite cosy at first sitting in between them. We sat in silence because of the engine noise and the wind howling round the cabin, it was getting really cold and the plane was not climbing very well with the pilot and three kitted out skydivers on board. It was taking a long time to get the height. Martin kept poking his head out the door to check on the wind direction by looking at clues like the airfield windsock and smoke from chimneys. I expect he was also looking at the views. Suddenly without a word or gesture he rolled out the door, I had this done to me before as a strange joke, the joker leaving others in the plane causing them to miss the drop zone target.

I was not going to fall for that trick so I quickly rolled out the door after him. This caused me to tumble and I found myself on my back looking at the plane. At that moment Mike's hands; then head and shoulders came diving out the doorway. To my amazement his right hand then shot out and grabbed the wing-strut and he hung on like a trapeze artist so I stayed falling on my back to watch what he was up to.

I was not surprised at his speed of movement or agility because he was a superb athlete. I saw the plane veer violently to the left in a semi-circle before the pilot recovered and flew off with mike still hanging on below the wing, what puzzled me was why he doing it?

I now had to turn my attention to what I was doing so I rolled over. Below me Martin was in free-fall still and to my horror below him was a bloody great town, it was Northampton. There were no open spaces to head for, it was pointless to open high and hope to drift away from the housing estates and huge expanse of shoe factories that appeared to be everywhere below us.

I opened my chute as I saw Martin going for his ripcord, thankfully the wind was light and we both had steerable 7TU chutes. With razor blades we had cut out five narrow panels at the back of the chutes and at each end a large cut which enabled us to turn the parachute around in order to see where we were going this also gave a forward speed of about 5mph).

I saw Martin land successfully on a road in a housing estate, I was still over an enormous factory with a glass roof. I had heard that shoe factories in Northampton had glass roofs but it has a different effect on the mind when you think you might be visiting them through the roof. I managed to land in the front executive car park but left part of my parachute on the roof, (the sleeve that encased the canopy to reduce the opening shock.) I did not bother to retrieve it for I could not imagine anyone climbing forty feet up over glass to get it for me.

I walked over the road to Martin who explained that he got so cold' and stiff he fell out the door of the plane, I replied that we were both lucky that we did not go through one of those glass factory roofs and end up as cold stiffs.

We got a taxi back to the airfield where Mike was waiting for us and over a cup of coffee he explained that as his head cleared the door he saw the town and grabbed the strut. Then he held on for over two minutes while the pilot flew back to Sywell Aerodrome; that was nearly five miles at 120 mph.

I believe that the area that Martin and I landed in was Moulton Park. That is not a wooded grassy park but a dense housing and business estate.

I BLEW IT

It was in the early 1960' that GQ Parachute Company produced a seven gore TU 28ft parachute in delightful colours and in an alternate chequered pattern. A number of the British Skydiving club at Thruxton purchased these parachute canopies. I chose a Gold and white pattern and I have a picture of myself under it when I tested it with a ten second delay free-fall.

On the next jump from 10,000 ft. After deployment I looked up and had a shock. It looked like a Kitchen-Colander! Every gold panel had blown out. I considered throwing my reserve chute but reasoned that it was very much like a colander and if you fill a colander with water it cannot get through the holes very fast. The same applied to the flow of air through the holes in the parachute so I felt confident to land on that very ragged chute. I was correct.

The reason it happened was that the gold dye degraded the nylon parachute material whereas the other colours never had the same effect. The GQ Parachute Company replaced the parachute with a red and black pattern.

Note. The 7TU was a favourite cut on the 28ft chute before the Para -Commander came on the market. The TU being cut out was the most that could be cut out safely. It meant 7 panels were cut at the rear of the 28 panel parachute.

The next short story is about a 9TU.

THE 9 TU.

When I was jumping at Shoreham Airfield having used my chutes I saw a packed chute and asked if I could jump it. The owner agreed but did not tell me that he had just cut out 9 panels!

On opening the front of the parachute started curling under, I gently pulled the front risers about 4inches and the chute collapsed into a roman candle. As I went for the reserve chute it cracked open again with such force one of my boots came off. I decided to just ride it down as it was! And not to try turning or even touch the risers. Luckily the wind was light and I landed on the edge of the field but my boot fell into a marshy area and I never found it. The owner of that chute had never jumped it and never did.

PARACHUTE DISPLAYS BY THE BRITISH SKYDIVING CLUB.THRUXTON.

17/JUNE/1961 Display at R.A.F. 20th Tactical Unit, Wethersfield, Myself, Tony Miller, Stan Anstee, Martin Griffith's. Martin had a malfunction and threw his reserve.

30/AUG/1961. Display at RAF. COTTESMORE, OAKHAM, RUTLAND. Ref, Battle of Britain Show
Note cost, Insurance 15 shillings, Petrol 280 miles £2.10.0

DEATH OF MIKE REILLY.

Mike was a founder member of the BPA and the first chairman. He was studying at the London School of Economics. He was a superb athlete and played water-polo. I tried this sport with him and found that I just did not have the energy required to play for half a game.

MIKE DIED DURING THE MAKING OF THE FILM 'THE WAR LOVER' ON THE 10th/JAN/1962.

The story was of a B17 pilot played by the actor Steve McQueen. A team was assembled from members of The British Skydiving Club at Thruxton.

On the 9th of January we all did three jumps in four hours, from the B17 onto Manston Airfield in Kent, this included the repacking of the seat types we were using for the film. Tony Miller threw his reserve when he could not find the ripcord to the seat type. Dennis Smith got concussion. I bent my Sternum on the large British harness box re-lease system.

On coming in to land on the last fateful flight I was in the nose cone. As the B17 hit the runway it jumped violently sideways, then as we taxied up to the hangers the undercarriage collapsed with the oleo leg going right up through the wing. Had it collapsed on the previous flight it is probable the fatal scene would not have taken place. Three B17s all started out from America for this film and they all ended up as scrap.

The story is on page 30 – The War Lover.

51

MODIFYING AMERICAN CHUTES. 1962

12/April/ 1962 I Started modifying American parachutes by simply cutting out panels with a razor blade and attaching control lines to the outside gores. My first was a American C9 to having two L shaped turning panels with a pyramid shape cut out centrally to give it a forward drive. I tested it and called it the Green Flyer. It had a reasonable forward speed that enabled students to move away from obstacles and it had a nice rate of turn. It was a popular modification.

B.P.A. 22th Apr 1962

GOODWOOD SPOT LANDING CHAMPIONSHIPS.
I did four drops 3 from 5,000ft and one from 7,000ft. The aircraft registration was G-ARCA. I was not placed in the finals.

17th JUNE 1962 PLYMOUTH AIR RALLY.

Parachute competition at DUNKESWELL.
Judge Peter Lang. Many military men were there including Sherdy Vatsndal and Charlie Shea-Symmonds. It was a pleasant day but there was a very fast wind.

Sgt Mick Turner of the Parachute Regt was the winner, with a rather nice large silver cup. I came 2nd with a prize of £5 and small silver cup. Regarding the final decent, Mick Turner and my-self were the finalists. Mick and I left the aircraft together.

I approached the target in front of Mick and decided to

turn the chute into wind to get a softer landing as it was a very fast approach. At that moment Mick Turner was shouting at me and taking the mickey of me for taking the easy option, as he came driving downwind to win the competition by crashing in.

Next day he showed me his leg, from the ankle to his hip was black and blue with streaks of yellow. I am glad I turned around and especially when years later I met him and he complained that his bones hurt when he drove the tractor on his farm.

LIVING

Life or existence
I want to enjoy this life
not just to exist.

Senryu.

NHS

Require heart surgery?
If you are obese or smoke
You might not get it

Senryu.

Think about it, as if you were a surgeon.

BRITISH SKYDIVING CLUB

MARTIN AND THE PERCIVAL PRENTICE.

A story about how the first parachute club to purchase its own aeroplane in the UK managed to do it.

I think it was in August 1962 that Martin B. was flying out of Thruxton aerodrome in his Percival Prentice G-AOKF. I asked him if I could jump from his plane before he set course for home, he agreed.

The Percival Prentice had been a basic trainer for the RAF, 1946 to 1943. Approximately 370 were built. As it was a low wing all metal monoplane I wanted to experience jumping from it. I was having problems hiring aircraft for my club British Skydiving Ltd. During the flight I told Martin that I would have liked to purchase the famous pilot Sheila Scott's converted Tiger Moth G-APAM. It had been converted to a four seater and just right for a pilot parachuting instructor and a student and had a good climb rate to 6000ft. It had a very strange name instead of Tiger Moth it was called a Jackaroo. Martin asked why I had not already purchased it, I explained that I did not even have the deposit.

We were at an altitude of 4,000 ft. when Martin took out a cheque, signed it and gave it to me without an amount written on it! Then said, "Buy it." He did not give me any if's but's or rules.

You have heard the story of the butterfly's flapping wings creating an updraft, which causes a thermal which creates a storm. Well, that loan to me for the deposit on that plane enabled me to create the British Skydiving Ltd business and change parachuting in the UK for ever.

As I climbed out onto the metal wing, Martin asked me to close the canopy. I did so and he then locked it with a Click-Clack noise. The finality put me in shock, I was locked out! It was like your wife locking you out of the house, the feeling was irrational and totally ridiculous. I am wearing a parachute and it was my intention to jump! I reasoned with myself for a moment then having settled my peculiar anxiety I turned to jump.

Normally one fell out the door or stood on a rubber stepping point on the wing and jumped backwards. But now I had a metal wing to walk on until the slip-stream blew me off the back of the wing (So I thought). I walked slowly and found it was no effort at all to stand erect and so I continued walking fairly slowly right to the tip of the wing.
Here I must tell you that I had tried rock climbing but found it scared the life out of me. Afterwards I found that when standing on bridges or any heights like cliffs, I felt that I was being drawn to the edge and sometimes I had to drop onto to my knees to stop going over the edge.

As I looked over the edge of the wing tip at the earth 4,000ft below; my heart jumped and my stomach churned for a second until I told myself to stop being silly and I dived over to enjoy my free-fall. The brain is sometimes irrational and indeed most complex.

EVENTS AND DATES
RELEVANT TO SKYDIVING AT THRUXTON.

12/AUG/1962 Helen Flambert had completed a course and had got to jump from 3,000ft at Thruxton. Her next jump was from 12,000ft with me at an RAF base show. The story is called 'The Shuttlecock.' I was holding on to her in the following manner, she held a spread position and I curled up in front of her holding on to her harness. So I was the weight and she was the feathers of the shuttlecock! This kept her stable and I was able to talk to her. When she said she was confident I let go of her. at around 6,000ft. The story is in my first book Dunce or Dyslexic.

08/SEPT/1962. I attended The Centre du Parachutisme at Chalon-sur Saone in France for a Skydiving course. I did six jumps the first day including packing the chutes. A sharp change from only eight jumps in a year in the UK.

25/SEPT/1962. BRIAN TAYLOR of The Parachute Regiment, died at Thruxton. Jumping from 3000 ft. He did not attempt to pull his ripcord. The story is in Dunce or dyslexic, I called it The Enigmatic Smile because he smiled sweetly at me as I gave him instructions as he stood on the wing which had really puzzled me.

1963 I opened a Parachute Club at Stapleford Tawney with Pat Slattery as Chief Instructor. Pat lived in NE London. Unfortunately it did not become viable and was closed. Story in Dunce or Dyslexic Thruxton Skydiving number (7).

1963. Skydiving Accounts. These accounts show that all British Skydiving members were required to join the British Parachute Association. The fees were included in their membership and course fees and then forwarded to the BPA. Not all clubs were insisting on this payment to join the BPA.

14/FEB/1964 Company name was changed to British Skydiving ltd. The company was formed on 25/OCT/1962 with the title Parachute Equipment (Surplus) ltd

1964 British Skydiving Ltd purchased an aircraft the Jackaroo G-APAM which was a converted Tiger Moth named MYTH 11 previously owned by the famous Aviator and Author. Sheila Scott. The cost was £725.0.0. To make price comparisons at that time a new jaguar E type was £2.200.

29/APR/1964 DAILY MIRROR article on Helen Flambert who started Parachuting at Thruxton with British Skydiving Ltd in 1962. The De-Havilland Rapide shown was hired.

JUNE 1964. BRITISH SKYDIVING purchased a De Havilland Rapide G-AKNN, called THE BROWN BOMBER cost £1.000.00. Then soon after this I had to replace an engine with a reconditioned engine at £1.000.00 plus fitting. To give an idea of value or cost comparison my Semi-detached 3 bed house, 'Wilmslow' with no central heating cost £2,200 in 1959.

Our De-Havilland Rapide was nicknamed the Brown Bomber because it was a shitty brown colour and perhaps because our female pilot kept spraying deodorant into the cabin at altitude especially if the skydivers had been eating beans at breakfast.

DEADLY COMBINATIONS Part B.

PARACHUTING & SKYDIVING.

Peter was a member of our Skydiving club at Thruxton. He had joined as a student and having done all his static line jumps had progressed on to free-falling. This was done in slow progression, first only falling free for five seconds then in increments of ten seconds also being watched to see if he could control his movements in the air without spinning out of control. Spinning can cause the blood to go to the head and cause the person to go unconscious.

He was proficient and was soon joining the more experienced skydivers in the British Skydiving Ltd Rapide aircraft to jump in sticks of eight jumpers and free-fall together. This is an amazing and exciting experience; it can be like ballet in mid-air. I find it difficult to express in words how it feels and the best a person with their feet firmly on the ground can get is by watching a quality film of it and then try flying in a specialized wind tunnel.

One cloudless fine day Peter joined a group of experienced skydivers in the Rapide and climbed high over the airfield. I was in the control tower talking to the Chief Flying Instructor. We watched the aircraft come across on its final run heading east towards and over the village of Thruxton. Whoever was spotting that day (Spotting means directing the pilot to the desired exit point) went too far to the South of the wind direction that would bring the parachutists floating back under their parachutes to the middle of the airfield. This does not matter much to experienced Skydivers as they can fly across the sky for some distance from high altitude, this was called "Tracking."

As the group left the plane they all started tracking northwards to get on the wind line.
The last to leave was Peter; he fell in the standard position for a few seconds and obviously observed the others moving away from him. He copied them, taking up the tracking position with his arms to his sides, legs and feet together, head up and a slightly arched back. This position was at that time was also starting to be used by Ski-jumpers.

I watched the leading skydiver open his chute followed by the others. At that moment I saw Peter put his head down and that caused him to somersault violently over and over a number of times. Eventually a parachute appeared and streamed out but it was too late as he hit the very high beech trees in the village of Thruxton.

I think he might have survived had he missed those trees. I also believe that he got carried away emotionally when he found that he was flying across the ground. He should have been watching his altimeter, not the others in front of him. He might have been waiting for them to open their chutes.

The extended time tracking across the sky would not have happened if they had been over the airfield. It looked as though he put his head down to read the altimeter on top of his reserve chute without bringing his arms forward to flare out. Or perhaps he looked down for his ripcord on the left side of his chest harness? He had left it too late to flare out and operate his chute. Putting his head down and somersaulting violently would disorientate him. He was attempting to track, which he had not been taught to do or try. Had he opened his chute at the normal height he would have drifted into open grass fields on the south side of the airfield. There was a slight chance that if he had been over open ground his chute would have opened in time as it was already streaming out, but he hit the top of the huge beech trees with the canopy and lines fully extended. A combination of small errors can equal a disaster.

TRUE PLEASURE

What is true pleasure
unadulterated joy
To come home each day

BPA. NOVEMBER 1962 CHANGE OF SECRETARY.
B.A.N. GREEN to K.R.C. LETTS.

Colonel Dare Wilson the chairman of the BPA. requested me to step down as Hon Secretary so he could appoint an ex-military gentleman K.R.C. Letts, who became the full time secretary in 1966. I did so as it was becoming much busier and I wanted to pay more attention to British Skydiving Ltd.

PARACHUTING (THE SUIT)

It was a beautiful sunny Sunday at Thruxton Aerodrome. The British Skydiving Club instructors were busy dropping student parachutists on static lines from the club Jackaroo aircraft G-APAM. It was a Tiger Moth converted into a four-seater.

Peter Lang arrived at the club; he had been my instructor for my first jumps at Fairoaks aerodrome, Nr Woking sponsored by the GQ Parachute Company. Peter introduced me to his wife, they had just got married. He worked for Aquascutum and was always immaculately dressed and this day he was wearing a beautifully tailored grey striped suit, white shirt and silk tie, I also noted the handmade shoes.

Peter asked me if he could despatch a student. 'despatch' did not mean causing the poor student physical harm but to travel in the aircraft and instruct the pupil when to jump. I agreed and he said he did not wish to jump after the student on this day but he borrowed a backpack parachute for safety reasons and donned it over his suit.

His pupil was to do a static line jump. His wife and I walked out to the drop zone in the middle of this huge grass airfield and arrived at the target area as the plane came overhead at 2,500 ft.

We could see the student climb out onto the starboard wing of the Jackaroo aircraft and then jump, rather quickly I thought. At the same time another chute opened on the port side. "Peter never said he was going to jump." I said to his wife as we watched the two descend. Peter came floating down quite close to us. It was a good example of spotting. I say floating because he was of light build. When he was close to us we could see that he did not have a helmet or reserve chute. His suit was in torn and his face and shirt slightly bloodied. "What happened," we chorused as he landed. He was not seriously injured but had numerous scratches. He and the student then explained what happened.

61

Peter had directed the pilot to the exit point and asked for the engine speed to be reduced then he told the student to climb out onto the wing. The student had to wait for the instruction to jump. As the student looked at Peter he saw Peter's parachute pack snag on the upper part of the open cockpit and pop the pack open.

He tried to tell Peter but could not because of the engine noise; he saw the parachute drifting out over the pilots head into the slipstream. Peter was shouting for him to jump and was oblivious of the danger he was in. The student very wisely decided it was time to leave, at the same moment Peter's chute was streaming out into the slipstream over the tail-plane and then it opened pulling Peter out of the aircraft. But not out of the door but through the fuselage, ripping out the tough laminated wooden door frame that was at least 30mm square in thickness. He must have partially travelled over the pilot. Luckily the chute slid off the tail-plane but the tail was damaged to the extent that the pilot could only make left turns, he landed awkwardly but safely. The pilot recovered after a couple of drinks but the repairs took a week. Peter's wife probably did not want to see another parachute jump but later Peter joined our team to do the parachuting for the Steve McQueen film THE WAR LOVER where we lost our good friend Mike Reilly.

THE FLAT

Who's knocking the door
I don't know. Where's the back door
Sorry, there isn't one

Senryu. Note. Young and dangerous days.

TO VALUE A MAN

To value a man, to find his worth or infamy
Number his friends, more than five, too many
A successful man is often quite a louse
Conversely with no enemies, a mouse
Remember where your family live and breathe
Friends! When you are in trouble they leave
Don't try and die a multi-millionaire
Just do your best in everything and care
If this is done and you try your best
Fate will always take care of the rest

MOTORBIKE

An old motorbike
is a man's best possession
or his enemy

Senryu.

I have always had motor-bike's, My first scooter was a Zundapp Bella which I kept falling off I think that was because of the small wheels.

My favourite was a 1955 Triumph Bonneville which I unofficially used in the Army Post Office. It could do 110mph so I got my job done quicker than the other guys that were pedalling rusty old heavy Army bikes.

I have had Vincent's, very hard to start. A 1960s Thruxton 500cc Velocette but that made my hands numb. A 1993 740cc Triumph Trident but found it a bit top-heavy. A 1997 ZRX1100 Outfit. Wow it is very fast.
My favourite now is a Honda CBF600F as it handles perfectly.

JOY

The joy of smoking
five members of family
they are all deceased.

Haiku. Poor them poor you (if you smoke.)

PEOPLES PERSON

President Zuma
A poor man of the people
has bought a Boeing.

Senryu.

PALS AND PUBS

I thought my life was quite normal
But now I am not too sure
I've never had a long-time friend, a pal

Was it because I never got drunk
or as I preferred female company,
I'd never choose to be a monk

I found most males moved with the money
So when things got tough, they flew
Like bees searching for the pot of honey

I've organized companies, café's and clubs
planes, boats and balloons. But in times
of stress they all disappeared to the pubs.

1st June 1964 BRITISH PARACHUTE ASSOCIATION

Chairman; Colonel R.D. Wilson.
Vice-Chairman; JR Trustram-Eve.
Hon Secretary, Group Captain W.S.Caster.
Treasurer; D.M.Pearson

Committee;
Sgt A.F. Charlton.
A.J.N Cole.
Mrs M. Denley.
Lt. E. Gardiner.
Brigadier G.C.A.Gilbert.
B.A.N. Green.
S/Sgt D.Hughes.
Mrs A. Lang.
Sgt J. McLoughlin.
J.E. Hogg
Sir Godfrey Nicholson, M.P.
D.M. Pierson.
A.W. Porter.
B. Porter.
Mrs T. Richard.
Doctor C. Robertson.
Sgt P.W. Sherman.
Group-Captain F.B. Sowrey, A.F.C.
Brigadier W.F.K.Thompson.
Sgt P.W.Turner.
Major T.W. Willans. (Dumbo Willans)

BRITISH PARACHUTE MAGAZINE

Note. The order form for the Sport Parachutist was to The Secretary General. B.P.A. Lower Belgrave St, London S.W,1.

Page 11 SIR GODFREY NICHOLSON
Parachuting at Thruxton.
Photos by B. Green.

B.P.A. MAGAZINE AND ARTICLES 29th June 1964 DAILY SKETCH. Article with pictures of JACKIE MCGOVERN aged 17 yrs. The UK's youngest parachutist she was trained at Thruxton. Her uncle Malcolm Critchell was an experienced Skydiver.

5/AUG/1964 TATLER MAGAZINE Page 251 JACKIE MCGOVERN aged 17 yrs. parachuting at British Skydiving at Thruxton .

5/AUG/1964 TATLER Pages 252/253 HELEN FLAMBERT exiting the aircraft over Thruxton.
The story is in the book Dunce or Dyslexic by Simpleton a pseudonym for Bernard Green.

SPRING 1965 SPORT PARACHUTIST

B.P.A Magazine Vol 2 No1
Page 16, The Thruxton Letter, Photo of B.Green exiting a Tiger Moth this was taken years earlier over Sandown Isle of Wight at 6,000ft when I was using the GQ Parachute No 352206.

APRIL 1965. British Skydiving club was established at Halfpenny Green, Aerodrome, Bobbington, Near

Birmingham. With MIKE WEST as Chief Instructor, New VW Van, all American parachuting equipment and the Jackaroo four seater aircraft G-APAM .

25th JULY 1965 Article full central page of SUNDAY MERCURY Showing Mike west and club members Christine Pearson and Carol Frith.

1966 A FRACTURED SPINE

1966. I fractured my spine in three places when giving a skydiving display in adverse conditions during an Air Display at Halfpenny Green. I decided to jump after stopping the other club members due to the high wind I was worried about losing the club due to not having enough members to make it viable. I thought I could encourage new members, it was a big mistake.

While I was standing on the wing of the Tiger Moth at the height of 5,000 feet and obtaining my position to jump from the aircraft. It looked as though I was on a helicopter as we were not making any forward progress at all. I was desperate to make the Halfpenny club a success. Stupidly this made me convince myself that the wind at ground level would be slowed down slightly. The story is in my book Dunce or Dyslexic and called A Broken Back. But what was not written was that I could not feel my legs and therefore could not drive, I desperately wanted to get home as I did not wish to be stuck in a Birmingham hospital. My car had a bench seat so club member Christine Pearson who lived near Winchester and did not have a driving licence sat beside me and worked the pedals and I steered all the way back to Farnham, Surrey, a distance of 150 miles.

THRUXTON CLUB.

1967 SHELL AVIATION NEWS (MAGAZINE)

Pages 12 to 16
Article on Skydiving at British Skydiving Thruxton written by John Meacock.

Pilot Hugh Scanlon was editor of the magazine. Hugh was ex RAF and was also did some piloting of the Rapide for us at Thruxton.

1967 BRITISH SKYDIVING Ltd. Company Accounts Aircraft running expenses of the DE-Havilland Rapide G-AKNN. £1,348.15.4. The original cost of the aircraft was £1,000.0.0. with 750 hrs use on the port engine. A reconditioned engine was required after 250 hrs. A reconditioned engine was good for only 1000 hrs, and cost £1,200 fitted. It was not possible to purchase a new engine. This plane had been an airliner in its heyday and could carry eight passengers to 12,000ft.

ACTIVITY

If you can think of something
And visualize it: you can realize it
If you have dream and think of a scheme
So take rough with smooth.

STORMS

Winter brings suffocating snow and slippery ice.
It's difficult to decide where to be
Hot summer hurricanes are never very nice.

A storm at sea is frightening to see
watching waves pile up then pound the prow
It's when on land; you desperately wish to be.

Ripping the canvas of your sails
Waves come crashing over the bows
as the wet wind howls and wails.

Tornados terrify townships without hinder
Searing, scoring, scattering a path
Turning terraces of timber houses into tinder.

Hurricanes harass and harm country and city dwellers
prized property and possessions are pulverized
Some residents remain safe in subterranean cellars.

CHILDREN

The child's innocent smile
Sparkling untroubled eyes
Made me pause, to think
about children for a while
when their minds are free.
Free from the trials and
tribulations they will face

THE BARRISTER

A chameleon can change its colours
as I see it, so can she
Educated, elegant poised and pleasant
not hoity-toity, mixes well with others

The eyes, soft brown, doe- like
walks with swift fluid motion
Hah, but wait, so does a snake
glide, until it rises for a strike

Warm, but when in hushed courtroom
that warmth turns to icy blast
like an arctic wind on your face
with an intent to create, an air of doom

Looking soft, like butter on a summer day
she cuts to the bone
as a butcher cuts a carcass
and lays the joints out on a tray

Feline like a cat with impassive face
that when on an attack
show the incisors of a killer
used with precision, for the Coupe de Grace.

Note.
I watched her perform in the courtroom.
It made me cry out involuntarily.
So I got escorted out of the courtroom.

POETIC ATTITUDE

I have atti-chewed
you have atti-tood
Neither can you say nyther
and continue with neether
We duel over shed-uel
you will fight for sked-uel
In lieu of saying Leftenant
you fight for the lootenant
Our garage is english Gaa-raj
yours a french version Garidj
We properly pronounce Toma-toe
You improperly say Tomay-toe
Chips, you have to Frenchy-fy
to an absurd French Fries, why?
The letter Z is not Zee
It is definitely Zed, you see
So Zebra is Zeb-bra
not silly Zee-bra
and Bouy is pronounced Boy
not Boo-ee, it's more like ahoy
Nuclear cannot be Nukil-ar
it's New-clear, is that clear
Iraq, irritably spoken as Eye-rak
is irrefutably in English, I-rack
I am not adverse to say Vayze
for there is not an R in Vase
No need for risible ree-search
I agree to differ, after my research.

I wrote this to send to my poet friend
Aesthete2000 in America.

BOB ACRAMAN

Robert was an educated, gentle gentile child
Only his family thought he was quiet, mild
But others knew he was precocious, wild
Entered the Army Parachute Regiment
Really that's not what his parents meant
They wanted a civilian, he would not relent

Athletic, army trampoline champ, a trier
Corporal in rank, he wanted to get higher
Reacted to RSM's abuse consequences dire
Actually lost his stripes to his superiors grief
Mangled RSM's finger with his set of teeth
And started Skydiving, much to his relief
Nigeria his home now, a General my belief.

Note. The part of the above poem about the RSM was when he was a corporal and the RSM wagged his finger at Bob's face while lecturing him on being untidy. Bob bit the RSM's finger so he lost his stripes.

Note. Robert was an extraordinary Skydiver, it was most probably due to him being excellent on the trampoline before starting skydiving.

I wrote this as an acrostic poem where the first letters spell out his name.

THRUXTON NEWSLETTER.

BRITISH SKYDIVING CLUB
14th August 1967

There were over 3,000 descents made at the British Skydiving Club at Thruxton in the five months up to 14th August 1967.

It was the popularity of having our own De-Havilland Rapide aircraft. Full time Parachute Instructors and a very good selection of American Parachutes with different modifications. Also the fact that there were no height restrictions and a vast amount of grass to land on that made Thruxton so popular.

According to BPA figures there were a total of 14,450 parachute descents made in England in 1966, nearly 3,000 of them at Thruxton.

THE THRUXTON NEWSLETTER.
14th August, 1967.
Toll House, Runfold, Farnham; Surrey

So far this year has proved to be, full of records. We have achieved the distinction of being the only civilian club to operate its own De-Havilland Rapide. G-AKNN. We were the first to own an aeroplane although not many of you will remember our Thruxton Jackaroo G-APAM. which although much maligned did a good' job in keeping parachuting going.

This year, to date over 3,000 descents have been made at Thruxton. 'It would appear that Jim Crocker has done a large proportion of them for in one weekend - he made

22 descents. Last year according to B.P.A. figures the total number of descents in the UK was 14,450. There is still plenty of room for improvement and if we are to keep the Rapide costs-down the more the better. I suggest every member should work on publicity, tell your local paper what a brave chap you are, "Local Boy rises to Great Heights'", and plummets down again.

The Rapide has flown over 50 hours since May but we will need approx.200 hours, a year to keep it going properly. She costs approx., £1,800 a, year without flying and then costs £12 hour to fly on top. In 1965 we flew 83 hours in Mr Dommetts Rapide and 78 hours in 1966. So you can see it is a gamble.

Here is a very rough break-down of costs involved:

STANDING CHARGES:

Cost over 3 years, incl. H. P. Charges approx.	£350
Insurance	£180
Hangarage & incidentals	£320
Annual certificate of Airworthiness	£800
Maintenance checks	£150
Total	£1,800

Therefore if we fly 150 hours the standing costs will be £12. 0. 0. per hour.

RUNNING COSTS:

Engine time, 800 hour engines are approx. £1,000each fitted, therefore per hour £2. 10. O.

Petrol consumption, 22 gallons per hour at *6/2d.* =£6.15.8.

One and half gallons oil per hour at 12/-= 18/-.

Spares and contingencies, average. approx. £2.0. 0.
£12 3. 8.

Standing Charges at 150 hours use= £12.0.0 per hr.
Running costs =£12. 3. 8. hour

TOTAL COST PER HOUR with 150 hours £24. 3. 8.

Therefore if we fly 150 hours this year without too many problems or bad debts we should cut even. It is up to you to stop any abuse or damage to the plane because you are paying for it in the long run.

COURSES. I wonder if people realize that they can join in on any of the midweek courses provided they have paid the club fee of £5 per year or £3 for half year or 5/- per day. Contact the office for further information.

SPECIAL COURSE. October 1st to the 15th inclusive
John Meacock and John Burgess are operating a two week course for all members static line basic and advance sky-diving for the above dates. All reservations to be booked at Runfold as soon as possible the number will be limited to 30 in all

BPA COUNCIL NOMINATIONS.

The Thruxton club members nominated the following people for the BPA Council John Meacock, John Harrison, Nick Grieve, John Cole and John Beard. 14th August 1967.

WHALE-BONE

Why use whale-bone
in horse saddle construction
when plastic will do?

Haiku poem.

MY WIFE KNITTED IT.

Skydiver Yewdell White.

Yewdell White a very unusual name and a very unusual man, he was from Portsmouth and I met him when he joined my Skydiving school British Skydiving Ltd. He was called 'Snowy' because of his white hair; he had no fat on his body. I would describe him as scrawny the reason was he was a keen cyclist. Snowy was a very helpful club member and helped in many ways. In 1966 I fractured my spine in three places while
jumping at Halfpenny Green airfield to advertise the relatively newly opened British Skydiving Club at this airfield. I had been a fool to jump as the wind was far too strong but I felt obliged to advertise the new club. I had moved our Thruxton Jackaroo aircraft there after we had purchased the De-Havilland Rapide aircraft for the Thruxton club.

When I was able to walk again I needed a way of exercising my spine, that was when I came across a double canoe for sale; It was a quite old canvas canoe but in excellent condition, lovingly made with laminated polished wood and double bladed offset paddles everything highly varnished. At this time Snowy gave up Skydiving and he joined me in paddling in lakes and up estuaries. It was good exercise but it did not have the adrenaline rush of Skydiving.

It was early in the year, about February when we decided to go to Bracklesham Bay on the South coast overlooking the Isle of Wight. I had swum there years before and knew that there was a steep shingle beach and then a sandy beach stretching out for miles, at low tide it is admirable and safe for children to swim.

We arrived as the tide was coming in with a stiff onshore breeze, the waves did not look all that big as we sat on the shingle. The shingle is kept from eroding by heavy wooden fences called groins that extend about 50 metres out into the sea. Without them the beach would be scoured away by the tides that rush in and out of Southampton, Portsmouth and Chichester harbours. My first wife Ann sat watching from the van, she could swim but was not a strong swimmer so never came in the canoe with me.

I said to Snowy; we will stay near the beach as we a not used to waves. He replied "OK, but I'm not wearing the lifejacket it is too cumbersome". So neither did I. The waves were only breaking on the shore so we agreed to stay close inshore, just beyond the breakers.

After launching which was quite easy we found the waves exhilarating as we were being lifted up and then sliding down into the troughs. We wanted to turn around and face the shore to run with the waves but we found that the waves were too close together for our long canoe. It looked to us that the waves were not so turbulent further out to sea so we paddled on out to sea. There we found the waves were getting bigger but we were unconcerned,

As we slid down the watery slopes we were shouting "Weeeh", and laughing. The wind whipped up a spray that stung our faces as we climbed each next wave. We came to a wave that was so steep that I had to place my hand on Snowy's back to stop him falling back onto me as his seat back-rest broke. I thought to myself, the canoe is over 15ft long and the wave is higher so we had better turn round. As we wallowed up the next wave and hurtled down the other side there was no chance to turn. The canoe dived into the following wave like a submarine. In a second we were sitting in the sea without a canoe; It never surfaced and was never seen again.

We looked at each other in amazement; but there was no fear at this point. We both grasped our long double bladed paddles. Then the next wave hit us and I nearly had my head chopped off by Snowy's whirling paddle. As the blades were opposed they spun like helicopter blades in the surf. I threw my paddle away and Snowy followed suit. We were now up the creek without a paddle or a canoe! And the creek was the English Channel. Although I knew there were no rescue facilities at Bracklesham Bay in those days, I decided to shout for help.

Waiting until a wave lifted me up on its crest I filled my lungs to shout but on seeing the beach houses apparently a mile away I sank back in a mixture of horror and despair. I decided that I could not swim that distance with my clothes on so I started stripping,

I thought Snowy was stripping also. It was easy to strip off the jacket, shoes, trousers, socks even pants but then I made a mistake, I unbuttoned my shirt as the next wave hit me and pulled the shirt behind my back and pinioning my arms behind me like a straightjacket. Luckily the next wave ripped it completely off me; I had neglected to unbutton the sleeve cuffs..

I started to swim after Snowy and saw he still had a big woolly jumper on, the water had stretched the sleeves and he was flopping along with an overarm action with the wet sleeves flailing. Flailing is an appropriate word because it looked like two medieval corn flails whacking the water. "Snowy, take that jumper off" I shouted. "I can't" he said "I will help you" "No I cannot take it off because my wife knitted it" he replied?

We swam silently side by side apart from the flop, flop of his sleeves and the crashing of the waves. I became slightly ahead of him. I did not realize that I had stopped swimming, but it became all quiet and calm. Oh, I am going to drown, my limbs were numb with cold. I thought about my family, they would find my body and there will be a funeral with lots of flowers. Oh, they might not find me and the crabs and shrimps will eat me! This realization surged adrenaline through my body.

From Snowy's point of view he saw me stop swimming and sink below the waves, he thought 'He has gone'. Moments later I came up thrashing along as if a shark was after me. I had already lost sight of Snowy when I submerged and I had presumed that the woolly jumper had caused him to drown. Reaching the beach seemed possible now; I could see hundreds of people standing watching. Surely someone can help me get to shore. But I could not see any activity, I was on my own. I got to within 50 metres of the steep shingle beach. The waves were breaking high onto the shingle, so it was high tide.

I then found myself standing on the sandy sea-bed, it was quiet, I had stopped swimming again and sunk down to the sea–bed. My arms were by my side, the water was very clear, and it was so peaceful, it is strange but I was not frightened; I thought my next breath will be my last,

79

I was not worried. I could feel the sharp sand under my bare feet and thought this is the last thing I would feel so I curled my toes up and down crunching the gritty sand. As I looked around for my last look, I saw seaweed flying past and stones rolling along the sea floor travelling to my right. Looking up I could see the waves curling overhead I put my hand up and it broke the surface. At that moment I recalled that when I was a child of eleven years I was taken to the north coast of Cornwall where close to the shore I saw a seal poking his nose out of the water and having looked at me submerged again and then a minute or so later popped up to have another look at me.

I thought, I cannot swim as my arms were paralysed with cold and my legs felt dead. But I pushed off and up with my feet and ankles and gaining the surface took a gulp of air. Then sinking down I could see that I had moved a couple of metres to my right. On my next imitation of a seal I saw that the wooden groin stretching from the beach was over to my right. Three to five pop-ups like this and I should get there. I am only seven or eight metres off the beach and there were hundreds of men and women standing on the beach watching and making no attempt to help.

I was about three metres from the groin when I saw my wife Ann the mother of our two children enter the water fully clothed and make her way hand over hand holding onto the groin. Nobody assisted her as she dragged me back to the shingle beach with waves crashing around us. Only then did strong hands pull me out of the icy water. I was laying there on my back absolutely starkers with people standing over me when I heard a woman's voice, "Oh he is naked," and she put a small tea towel over my private parts! I swung my fist at her but it was totally ineffective. I said to her "You would watch me drown but to you my naked torso is disgusting". She walked away.

I vaguely remember a vicar Bless him, that got me into his warm caravan and I think I drank four tins of his tomato soup. I thought that Snowy had drowned but that evening I got a message that he arrived on the beach about a mile away to the east. We never found the canoe but I did not wish to see another one. I am not sure of the number of years that passed after this event but Snowy died of cancer. Before he died he arranged a party and invited all his family and friends so he could say goodbye. It lasted for days. It was a pleasure to have had his companionship.

My first wife Ann bore me three lovely children but we divorced and separated in the 1970s. I must commend her bravery in entering that icy water to save me when dozens of healthy young males just stood watching.

There's nowt so strange as Folk.

Note. There is a poem about this event in my book Dunce or Dyslexic called Copying a seal.

THE PLACID SEA

Under the surface of that calm placid sea
Seemingly a safe place for you and me
All creatures live in fear of being another's meal
It's not a safe place on the sunny surface
for a soft skinned person of the human race
to sharks looking up, they think you are a seal

Below there are long translucent stinging strings
Squid with sharp beaks and other clingy things
also torpedo shaped killers with toothy jaws
Others lay very still and quiet and wait
like the Angler fish with wiggly worm bait
and Stonefish that suck victims into maws

Even the gentle whales you might go to see
wallowing on vacation in the Southern sea
kill and eat squid, krill and lots of little fish
Doggone it, only the Dugong or Manatee
it seems will not eat or harm you or me
but crabs find our dead a very tasty dish.

THE SEA.

Desirable
unobstructed seaside view
killer when incensed.

This was written by the American poet Aesthete2000.

GIN PALACE

Calm sea, only ten yachts
A thousand in the harbour
What are they used for?

Note. I had a yacht, but I sailed it, so you need not answer my question.

Haiku.

SHIPS

Build ships higher still
They turn over more easier
Income is higher

Senryu

Note. There is approx. thirty feet below water and hundreds of feet above! If you jumped from the top decks of these modern ships you would most probably break your bones. I was in the Merchant Navy and my first ship was top heavy and rolled side to side a lot. Modern ships have stabilizer fins which tempt the shipping companies to build them higher and higher. What happens when they stop working?

DREAMS

If you work hard, it can and will happen
If you just laze around and think of gloom
You will end up dozing dopily to your doom

FAME AND SHAME

When a celebrity gets a name
in their quest for fame
Social drinking is the start
then so called soft drugs take part

Doctors and agents encourage their use
and the star then sinks into drug abuse
It is akin to riding on a runaway train
when constant rehearsing is a strain

Taking pills to sleep or keep awake
to promote energy other drugs they take!
Then they start to slide into deep decline
until they hit the end of the line.

It seems that once in the limelight
celeb's cannot quietly slide out of sight.

SAD SENRYU

Only a male moron
would pay to shoot a black rhino
to feel a Big Man

BOB ACRAMAN

I have always likened people to animals mentally putting them into a category and treating them likewise. There are plenty of snakes and rats and boring sheep. Bob was in the big cat family, a Cheetah, very athletic and with a devilish sense of humour.

He was one of my favourite characters that I had met in the Parachuting-Skydiving fraternity. I first met him when he turned up for a course at the British Skydiving club. He was a corporal in the Parachute Regiment and I was informed by others that he was an Army Cross country champion and expert on the trampoline. His trampoline skills soon became apparent in his fast assimilation of the art of Skydiving. He impressed me at a very early stage by passing me in free-fall standing upright to attention and saluting me as he went past.

To illustrate his humour, apparently on one of the Rapide flights he realized that the new students were lost in their own thoughts. He climbed outside and hanging on the roof pressed his face against the window. When the unlucky student came out of his reverie and decided to look at the view, he got a shock thinking he was looking at the devil. Well he did have a devilish humour. One day I noticed he had lost his stripes so inquired as to why. His Sergeant Major was telling him off for some reason and was wagging his finger in his face. Bob bit the offending index finger! It was not long before he got his stripes back. One thing was certain if you picked a fight with this wildcat then you would get bitten.

One memorable moment was when I was checking all the Parachutist's kit when they were getting into the Rapide aircraft. Bob marched up, gave me an exaggerated salute and said, "Ready for inspection Sah". He was not wearing the club equipment! I asked him about it and he said he had purchased it. It was an American B4 rig with a C9 canopy, of the type we were using. He was wearing overalls with the knees ripped out and hiking boots with metal lace up hooks. I pointed out that it had been known for rigging lines to catch in those boot hooks and hold you dangling upside down. I then saw that someone had tampered with the harness he was wearing. The harness could under the opening shock slide through the buckles.

I told him a Frenchman had been killed a week earlier when the two halves of his harness had come apart. Bob went white and started to walk away, I said "Bob it is not good enough to be a good Skydiver, you must look good also!"

The following week he turned up with all brand new kit and asked to purchase a pair of French Paraboots that I was retailing. I fitted him out and he promised to pay later. Weeks went by and although he paid for his flights at the club he did not pay me for the boots.

I was running two cafes at the time, The Milk Bar in the Borough of Farnham and a transport cafe called Alf's at Runfold. We used to get a lot of Para's in there as they marched back to Aldershot after parachuting into Hankley Common at Tilford Surrey. I decided to telephone Bob's Commanding Officer in Aldershot three miles away. I explained who I was and said something like this, "Look this chap in your Regiment owes me for a pair of parachuting boots, It's a bad show and not good for the Regiments name." He just said, "Leave it to me!"

I thought that he would speak to Bob and then take it

out of his pay. In the afternoon I was working on the café counter, there were about fifty lorry driver customers in the cafe when I saw an army jeep swing into the car park with two Redcaps (Military Police) sitting in it with Bob squashed between them. They jumped out and marched him into the cafe much to the amusement of the customers.

The Military police said nothing but Bob said "You Bastard. "I replied "You owe me the money don't you?" He shrugged; paid and then with a smile was marched out to the jeep. To my surprise he never mentioned it again. The next surprise that he gave me was after I closed the British Parachute Club. I closed the club because the flying hours on the Rapide were not being recorded correctly and that could have ended up causing a fatal accident.

CLOSURE OF BRITISH SKYDIVING LTD

It was months before I could walk properly again following my parachuting accident when I had fractured my spine in three places. This was followed by some very painful physiotherapy.

On a fine summer day I turned up at Thruxton to see how things were going. There were nine parachuting instructors at the club now that were earning some money on a part time basis from teaching, hiring out the equipment, packing the chutes and getting free jumps when they followed out the students.

When I arrived I saw the De-Havilland Rapide at the end of the runway so I parked close by it and went to the open door. I could see that there were only seven parachutists on board and it could carry eight.

"Any room for me" I asked, "Sure jump in." was the reply. There was always a fast turnover of students as only about ten percent continued jumping after their initial one jump course. There were no club instructors on this flight as they were all qualified skydivers.

As the aircraft climbed above three thousand feet one of the men started collecting money. He came to me and said "Half a Crown". I asked "What is that for" and he replied. "There are eight of us, we give the pilot the £1 and he knocks off a quarter of the flying time, Good eh?" I gave him the two shillings and sixpence. I did not wish him to know that I was the owner of the plane, as I did not have a parachute! The pilot could not see me.

When the plane landed I told the pilot he would not fly the plane again. I then got the Club Parachute Instructors together and told them I knew what was going on, that the pilot had been taking bribes to reduce their flight times and thereby reducing the cost of the flight to all of the high flying skydivers wanting to go to 10,000ft which took one hour of heavy flying time. It did not take place on the short flights when dropping the students on Static Lines from 2,500 ft.

I started to explain to the parachute instructors that the Rapide engines were only good for 1,000hrs flying time and then they had to be replaced. What was happening was extremely dangerous. I had previously printed the costs involved in the club newsletter on the 14/Aug/1967.

I knew what I was talking about as I had been on the Rapide when a previous engine cut out, luckily there were only four of us passengers on a jolly and only a half tank of fuel otherwise we would have ended up with the lions. We were flying past Longleat House at the Safari Park and we were only at rooftop height, I was looking at the statues that are on the roof at that moment the port engine coughed and lost power.

The pilot at that time owned his own Rapide and being very knowledgeable carefully kept it going by reducing the revs. I looked out the door at the lions and then realised we were in a valley, we only just cleared the trees and limped back to Thruxton. That engine was at around 950 hrs and I replaced that engine at a cost of over £1,000 plus engineer's time.

With a full load of kitted parachutists it would have been a different matter. There have been a number of incidents since when parachutists have been killed when engines have failed on take-off. I was explaining that due to this cheating taking place by the people wanting to jump from the higher levels. The engineers and I would think that our Rapide engines had 750 hrs use but actually they would be at or beyond 1,000 hours and in a critical state, a very dangerous state.

At around this point one of the very active skydiver instructors said to the group "Pubs open boys, let's go". This was said knowing that I do not drink alcohol and did not like going to the George pub in Thuxton village. Considering the danger that I had outlined and that there was no indication of an apology or show of intent to change matters I decided that I could not operate the aircraft with such a disregard for safety.

They probably felt that I was financially too committed and that I could not close the club. They were also taking advantage of my absence due to my spinal injuries.

This made up my mind to close the operation immediately as I did not wish to be held responsible for nine deaths, I had already attended an inquest and did not wish to attend another.

Within a week the Rapide G-AKNN was sold to the Royal Marines and they kept it at Dunkeswell Airfield but I understand it was totally damaged by sheep climbing all over it and urinating and defecating inside it. Perhaps the light brown colour made them think it was a special toilet for them

1968. Sadly the Jackaroo Aircraft. G-APAM had also been sold due to the Halfpenny Green parachute club running at a loss. I went back to running my transport café business ALF'S CAFÉ on the A31 road at Runfold. Also I became a Commercial Hot Air Balloon Pilot which was a tremendous amount of fun and excitement.

SATISFACTION

I am relieved
I feel an emptiness
I went to toilet.

BOB ACRAMAN, THE BUYER

Bob was now a Skydiving Instructor. I was in my cafe with a queue of about ten drivers that were buying breakfast at about £2.50 a time. Bob appeared at the back of the queue and shouted. "Do you want to sell your parachutes and kit to me?" I replied "Yes it is all in my house down the road, my wife Ann will show it to you." He came back a short time later and agreed to pay

£3,000.00 much to the curious looks of my customers. Bear in mind that my house cost me £2,200.00 in 1960.

I did wonder how he raised the money but he did and he bought himself out of the Army at the same time to set up his own Skydiving school at Thruxton and he made a great success of it. But eventually the airfield owner stopped the parachuting to develop motor racing. When I next saw Bob in the cafe he told me he was a General in Nigeria teaching parachuting and Air cargo despatching techniques. Later I heard he owned a Nightclub out there. As I said, he is a fighter; a big cat! a cheetah, tough and fast.

THE CHILD

Such innocence requires real care
Sweet trust that we are born with
is sadly very quickly lost forever
Though necessary in a world where
delicate things are ruined, crushed.

TIM BETTIN, THE SKYDIVER

Free-fall did not take his life
it was everything to him
He was wed to it, like a wife
In heavenly blue skies
he flew for precious seconds
Only falling, say earthbound guys

When Skydiving, time stands still
space and air, a gymnast's delight
To use the parachute needs iron will
Never angry, I've never met anyone
like Tim, disk jockey, sold fireworks
an adult child having lots of fun

Dived into the depths of the sea
always looking at life's creations
with such passion and childlike glee.
We bounced Balloons off each other
sliding over and through the clouds
Skydived through them, with no bother

He joined an Army Display team
a severe oscillation while on the chute
The acute angle ended his dream.
His wit, delivered with a cheeky smile
and thoughtful sparkling big brown eyes
will stay in my thoughts for quite a while.

Note. Tim was with me in my balloon flight over London. I've put some photos at the back of the book. By chance we landed in a field behind Tempest Avenue, at Potters Bar. This is where the L31 Zeppelin crashed after being shot down by Lt Wulstan Tempest.

PART 2

AUTOBIOGRAPHICAL

STORIES AND POEMS

THE ENGLISH DAME

The English Dame, when out on the street
of Badshot Lea, decided to eat brunch
of potato inkhorn and egg instead of lunch
With a loaf of bread and glass of mead
She mused; she was in debt no money
but had chattels; therefore no need to worry
A Scot came by. in his local dialect said "Hello"
gis a kiss for tea," she replied but wasn't rude
" Take away your merry riddle, wicked wee dude"
Then he, lifting his plaid kilt
saying "What an unfriend, Ok Bye y 'all"
Showed her his doobry and arse, what gall.

By Simpleton on Dec 24, 2011. © Bernard Green

I am proud of this little poem as it was my entry for the prestigious David Crystal poetry competition in the Daily Telegraph. On the 06/12/2011. I was advised that I was on the short list of fourteen entries and my poem was be published in the Daily Telegraph. The poem had to be no more than 100 words using at least 25 words from David Crystal's list of English words.

The next poem is about Farnham which is the nearest town to my childhood village of Runfold. I went to `East Street School in Farnham. Followed by attending Heath End Secondary Modern.

FARNHAM SURREY

Farnham was once a farmer's market town
they brought their sheep and cattle to sell
All such wonderful sights and country smell
Years ago it was called Fernham
because of the abundant ferns that grow
They are still there in parks and hedgerow
Just leave your land untouched
And the ferns will quickly spread
If the animals eat it, they will be dead
The Monks created Frensham Ponds
for fish, it took many years of toil
They built roads and cultivated the soil
living in seclusion in Waverley Abbey
where they farmed the land and did pray
Also managed the waters of the River Wey
imported fine furs from Russian traders
carried in bales up the river Wey by boat
Traded, bred cattle sheep and goat
They became too powerful for Henry VIII
and he required money for his wars
He stole their wealth and closed their doors
Down the river, Tilford with its Roman Bridges
a Ford where children swim, it must be seen
They have a cricket pitch on the village green
Then move on to see the Devils Punchbowl
where a highway was removed for you
So you can peacefully enjoy the view.

THE LANCHESTER CAR

I was born in 1934 at Runfold, Farnham, Surrey. My father Alfred Edwin Ambrose Green owned a small cafe which started life as a garden shed and was called ALF's Cafe. It was a favourite stop for charabancs and holiday-makers as it was half-way between London and Portsmouth. The village consisted of a petrol station with three pumps owned by Mr Timperley who in size and manner acted like the Officer in charge of TV's Dad's Army. He was in charge of the local Home Guard. There was a Post Office Mr and Mrs Jerome lived there and there was a public house called The Jolly Farmer.

My father acquired a second hand Lanchester car, perhaps nobody else wanted it as it only did about twelve miles to the gallon and there was strict petrol rationing at the time. It had a six cylinder engine, a glass division which separated the passengers from the chauffeur and a speaking tube to direct him. It was a stately car with long bonnet and a Rolls-Royce looking radiator, flat windscreen and a huge box of a body.

Father decided to take the family to Ilfracombe in Devon in this car. The baby's pram went in the back then there were my two sisters and 'Avril Westbrook' a young girl from next door, seven of us. Her father was foreman of Ebenezer Mears Sandpit in Runfold. He had five girls and wanted a boy but he got killed in an accident in the pit before the boy was born. This happened when due to his kindness he was serving someone after closing time as a favour.

I particularly remember this trip as before we got to Ilfracombe it became dark and about ten miles from our destination the engine stopped. My father lifted the flat side of the bonnet and laid me between the bonnet and the large front wheel mudguard. This cradled me quite comfortably and I had my right arm wrapped around the large headlight. Luckily it was a warm night. I was then instructed to constantly tickle the carburettor float needle as my father continued to drive to Ilfracombe. Health and Safety would interfere now.

We stayed for a few days at a little hotel in the town and I saw anemone's for the first time in the bay. There are not any there now. While we were there a boy jumped over over a wall but he was killed as it was the seashore cliff in the other side of that wall That taught me an early lesson to look before you leap.

PETROL

Here is a warning. Unfortunately a lot of people and I was one of them that think that petrol burns very quickly and brightly. But it explodes. Think about it, it explodes in car engines. It explodes when contained in any space and it catches many people out. It was 1949 and I was fifteen years of age. My parents had purchased a large Victorian house called Holmefields at Whiteways Corner in Runfold , Farnham, Surrey. The Army had requisitioned this house during the war and it had been empty for a while. At each corner of this twenty-one roomed house the builders had installed huge rainwater collection tanks, but during the period the house had been empty someone had tipped rubbish into one of the tanks that for some reason was totally dry.

The top of the tank was a concrete slab about six inches thick and probably nine feet across, piled on top and about four feet high was a rockery consisting of large rocks and soil. I thought that I would do a good service by burning the rubbish, so I poured at least a gallon of petrol into the open manhole.

I knew it would go 'Woof' when I lit it and expected a flame to leap up from the open manhole so I screwed up balls of news-paper, lit them and threw them from the doorway of a building. I kept missing the hole. While doing this I did not notice my brother and adopted brother approaching from around the building. As the flaming paper finally went into the hole I saw them arrive, at the same moment there was a tremendous Bang and the concrete lid and rockery went up into the sky.

For a second there was a clear space beneath this flying concrete and debris and I could see my brothers running like gazelles. They did not stop running until they nearly went over the top of the nearby sand-pit quarry. The concrete and approximately two tons of rockery came raining down, luckily without too much damage but my brothers never forgave me; I don't know why.

CHERRY BLOSSOM. (Adult)

She was attractive, motherly, matured
I am the chauffeur, taking her to town
my attitude, stiff upper lip, self-assured
It was hot, the month of May
Cherry blossom trees line the road
"I've always wanted," I start to say

"So have I," and my cheek she kissed
What I had intended to say, was
I always wanted to live in a road like this
Her hand delved between my thighs
I'm driving at forty miles an hour
"I knew you wanted me," she sighs

My brain spun, I did not believe my ears
split seconds later, I knew
as I crashed and crunched the gears
Trying to concentrate on the road
as she massaged between my thighs
I thought might as well unload

Speed increased, as did my spinning brain
legs stiffened, pleasure, pressure on the gas
arrangements made to meet up again
It was a short but most pleasant affair
she was exciting, fiery, inviting, but
we both knew it could end in despair

An unexpected ending due to a misunderstanding. I was nineteen, she delightfully older.

LOVING AND MARRIAGE

It trips off the tongue too easily, often
Love is such an easy word to say
It's used to describe many things
Love my car, have a lovely day

We show love in many different ways
loving our family, horse, dog, or cat
And when blessed with children
we love them lots, we all know that

When first you meet, it's all visual
chemistry, pheromones and genes
Later you will enjoy your spouse
in other ways and different means

Love can be of many types and shades
It will be varied powerful and strong
like Jacob's coat that he wore
Sometimes sweet as a skylark's song

Love can be confusing, for with love
anger can be close at hand
Marriage can bond you tight together
with meeting of the minds, it's grand

The passion of a lasting clinging kiss
can be replaced by a silent look
Which will be understood by you
and the meaning could fill a book

This world is meant to be chaotic
stress and upset is the norm
to test your strength and your will
Together you can find peace and form

Marriage, an act, so strong a deed
and sanctified by the Lord above
We gather in the house of God to
share this, the highest bond of love

We gather here to witness marriage
not in fear and trepidation.
The next hymn, Jesus loves you
Sung with feeling, love and elation

Here we have love in its finest way
Two persons on this stage, in an act
with faith in one another, to marry
and prove it in front of all, in fact

We'll sing, Love in its many forms
love of parents, sisters, brothers, wives
We all know of these different loves
that affects us all, in all our lives

Your life will not run straight and true
like a bullet or Channel Tunnel train
it'll twist and turn with ups and downs
but order will come in your domain

Then you will laugh, not cry when you
find the moth has ate your woolly hat
You will giggle and share the joke
and say, "I hope he enjoyed eating that,

When your wife sets out your tasks
those jobs to do when she is going out
Be content, when it was woman's work
to do the dishes, machines were not about

And when your dear wife's snoring
keeps you wide awake all the night
think not of waking her, but listen
and to its music, think of words to write

FELINE FUN

Do you value me?
Hubby, you're a lump of gold
an inert object!

A Senryu poem.

THEY SAW WARSAW

Israel knows of Siege
They saw the Siege of Warsaw
Starvation and Death

Note. Warsaw Oct 1939-May 1943.

Senryu

NAGGING

If you think your wife is always nagging
or seems to be
and your love for her is flagging

Before you walk out the door
Consider this!
you might not have been loved before

Parents might have been too busy working hard
to put food on the table
while you were playing in the yard

Now the loving wife worries about your health
and your well-being!
Worrying about you, not your wealth

So think carefully about the words she uses
What is it all about
Your beer belly, smoking or other abuses

Are you doing things like helping in the house
or saying that that's the women's job
Pretending you are tired and acting like a louse

You had better ask yourself, is she right
don't make excuses
Mine is unfortunately. Oh always be polite.

You might have been brought up as a male
chauvinist pig like me, but times are changing
Divorce lawyers are spinning a different tale

WINTER WOOLIES

The Nepalese arrived from overseas
as the leaves were shed from the trees

Without suitable warm thick winter clothes
their slim bodies froze from nose to toes

New was too expensive, they all concurred
So they walked for miles quite undeterred

Far and wide across countryside, to Car Boots
In pursuit of coats, hats suits and furry boots

Their original colourful appearance in apparel of Nepal
will submerge slowly, until they are not seen at all

Note. The Gurkha soldiers were based in Aldershot,
Hants, for many years now many families live there.

ARMY DAYS

This next story is about when I joined the Army, I know it is not in a proper sequence of events but I like writing about people and when you meet strangers especially if you are training or introducing them to a new experience you must be very careful about their reactions.

When teaching parachuting there were quite a few times when I politely suggested to the student that they take up a different sport due to different reasons.

SAPPER GILLFINAN

When I joined the Army for three years' service in 11/03/1954 I was posted to No 9 Training Regt Royal Engineers Southwood Camp, Cove Nr Farnborough Hampshire. This was very fortunate as my family only lived ten miles away.

I was a volunteer but most of my companions had been forced to enlist for two years for National Service. We were billeted in a wooden hut called a Spider, so called because it had a central wing for toilets and showers. Leading off this wing were six large rooms. In each room were housed twenty men, I call them men but at eighteen years old some of them cried themselves to sleep. And more than one told me they missed their mummy

We were not addressed as people or even humans, we were numbers. I was 22996966 or called Sapper Green, which sounds slightly derogative, but was a term used in the First World War for men that dug shafts or tunnels under the enemy lines. Then they filled them with explosives to blow the enemy to eternity or sometimes themselves in the process.

We were housed by name which meant I had a chap with the surname Gilfinnan in the bed next to me. The rooms were controlled by a Corporal whose responsibility was to teach us how to behave like unthinking robots and Army drill, that's marching. He was also responsible to ensure we kept everything clean and polished which became ridiculous.

I was forced to clean the front concrete steps with my toothbrush, and cut the grass with my issued penknife. The rooms were heated by coal fires and the coal buckets had to shine like silver. You will find it difficult to believe but I had to white-wash a pile of coal on one Brigadier's inspection.

Gilfinnan was a conscript I never knew what part of England he came from. His accent was so broad nobody could understand him, so I was never able to have a conversation with him. He was also seemed averse to washing, the problem was that if anyone did not reach a certain standard we were all punished by extra drill and loss of privileges. So some of the chaps got hold of him one night and scrubbed him with floor brushes and cold water.

One night I saw a large mouse in the room so I bashed it with my boot, thinking it dead I put it into G's left boot as a joke. In the morning I watched him put the boot on expecting him to react but he did not so I assumed the mouse had escaped. At the end of that day and a ten mile route march, 'G' took his boot off and peeled a very flat mouse off the bottom of his sock. Perhaps he had no feeling, no nerves?

Two days later we were herded in groups of five into a small wooden shed that had wire over the window. We were told to keep calm and not rub our eyes, after closing the door the sergeant sprayed tear gas into the shed. After a minute that seemed like an eternity, the door was opened and some walked and other staggered out crying. I could hear screaming and Gilfinan was trying to climb the netting over the window, the sergeant had to go into the shed and pull him off, he was like a gecko stuck to the wall. The next exciting episode was firing a Royal Enfield 303 rifle for the first time. I knew that the recoil would be fierce, as I had used a 12bore shotgun. We had already seen how the recoil (The backward thrust of the bullet leaving the barrel.) It made the shooters shoulder blade move back by inches.

"Pull the gun hard into your shoulder the Sergeant advised Gilfinnan." But the silly sapper decided to throw the gun away as he pulled the trigger, resulting in it coming back into his face. The result was a bloody mouth and severe bruising.

Our next joint adventure was manoeuvres when we were taken to a large lake near Guillemont barracks, Cove. This was to take part in a mock battle. We assembled on the beach of the lake and were issued with 303 blanks these are cartridges without the killing part, the copper clad bullet. Instead there is cardboard wadding, which I knew could be dangerous at close range. We were told to run up the hill across the deep heather to the trees and thick bushes where the enemy were waiting. I deliberately held back and sure enough when our group were yards from the rhododendron bushes they got peppered with cardboard wadding, some hard enough to draw blood.

At lunchtime we were issued with Thunder-flashes

which were very big banger fireworks to simulate hand grenades. We were warned that it could blow our hand off if it exploded while still holding it. We were then told that we were to lay in hiding in the heather while the tanks approached from the East side of the valley. I said, "Sir, I do not wish to be run over by a tank."
He replied "The tanks are imaginary." This was not very realistic training!

We were left to eat our packed lunch. Gilfinnan held his Thunder-flash and said "Is this how you light it? Then he drew the striker across the top, it is like striking a match on a matchbox. There was a stream of sparks and a fizzing sound. I rolled over and ran, so did the others. I then turned to see he was still holding it, then as he let it drop. It exploded at his feet, he was unhurt.

When firing the Bren gun which was truly an accurate gun and extremely well made weapon, that had no recoil. Gilfinnan started spraying the ground four feet in front of the barrel. The bullets sprayed across the 500 yards of ground then he emptied the magazine destroying the number 16 wooden sign which indicted the target below it that he should have shot at.

The final and most interesting event happened at the short distance firing range. This is where the Sergeant was to instruct us in firing the Sten-gun. This gun was for clearing streets and houses, clearing meant killing in Army terminology. I have read that this gun only cost two shillings and sixpence to make, that was one eighth of the old English pound of twenty shillings. The Sten gun looked like bit of old pipe welded together and did not have a recoil because it had a big spring inside. This absorbed the shock and reloaded the next bullet all in very quick succession.

Gilfinnan was in front of me as always. He was instructed to fire one round (bullet) into the bank of sand about thirty feet in front. He was clearly told to release the trigger after one shot, but he kept his finger pulling on the trigger. There were about twenty bullets in the magazine. I saw him start to turn to his left at the same time crying "Sergeant-Sergeant." I quickly stepped behind him and stayed there behind him as he turned ninety degrees. All the other recruits hit the ground as he emptied the magazine in a hail of bullets, it was a miracle that nobody got shot.

Can you imagine being in a real war zone with this young man? It was no surprise to me that he disappeared from our unit shortly after this.

POWER.

If I have a gun
I can rule everyone
Unless they have bombs

Senryu

CONSUMPTION

If the world consumed
like Americans consume
We would need three world's

Haiku.

DRIVING DINOSAURS

My first adventure with a mechanical dinosaur was in northern USA when I rented a car at a hotel. I asked for a compact car. I was given the key and went to the car park with Helen my 14yr old daughter. We just could not find a small car. It eventually dawned on my daughter to tell me that it was a brand new 1974 Chevrolet Impala four door sedan. This was full size 8th generation car with a V8 engine and a top speed of 103mph. length 5657 mm. 10.1 mpg.

Setting of in this fantastic car, the road was free of traffic, very boring and straight also there were no trees bushes or fence posts. I said to Helen, "That is how shoddy this car has been made; the speedo needle has fallen off." I showed her the needle lying at the bottom of the speedometer dial. She sat silent for a moment then said "Dad, take your foot off the pedal."

I did and the needle jumped back up. I was doing well over 100mph and did not know it. So much for being shoddy! A few moments later we went over a hump back bridge and there was a Cop, he stopped us and asked "Where's the fire buddy?" I put on my best Queens English, British not New York Queens and explained I was getting used to this wonderful car before I hit the next town. He let me go with a kindly warning. We drove from Calgary to Vancouver, visiting Johnson Falls, Athabasca glacier and stayed in log cabins. That was the best car journey I have ever had.

In 1987 when I was aged 53, I discovered that my Mother had a brother in the USA. Her father had been an alcoholic, and at the age of 12yrs she was sold into service to a wealthy English family, as an under-stairs maid. Within two years she was diagnosed as having Tuberculosis and was sent to a sanatorium, where she was incarcerated for two years. She had lost contact with all her family, but understood that her brother had emigrated on a £5.00 passage to the USA when he was 16 years of age. She had not heard from him at all for 63 years.

I traced him to Kansas City and phoned him, of course I addressed him as Charles Saunders-White, he replied. "You must be from England as no-one has called me Charles for over Sixty years."

The following year I Travelled to Kansas City, Missouri and was surprised to find that he was a successful Time and Motion expert. He had developed programmes for the American Milk Marketing board and The Coal board. I stayed with them for three days and then invited Charlie and his wife Ruth to England.

When I was in Kansas City I was amused by the fact that Charles still drove to his Skyscraper office in an old green Morris Minor of the type that was imported into the USA from the UK from 1949 to 1971. Its cost new was £382.00. Its top speed was 58mph but Charles never drove faster than 30mph. Nor would he clean or polish it. At the office he would hand the key to the doorman who would park it for him.

One day while Charles was at work, Ruth said she would take me to The Golf Club for lunch. She opened the double garage doors and jumped into an enormous yellow open Muscle Car. I am sure it was Pontiac GTO convertible with a 5.4l engine. These cars were built from 1964 to 1974. I never had time to look at it, she roared out of the garage like Cruella De-Ville in the film 101 Dalmatians.

Sitting low in the seat with a tremendously long bonnet, I could not see the road for some distance in front of the car. We roared down the single lane tarmac road, the engine sounding like a straight six cylinder un-silenced engine on a Tiger Moth aircraft.

As she changed gear she shouted over the noise of the engine "This car has got a Hurst Shift." I had no idea what she was talking about. And I did not ask because I could see there were six children sitting in the middle of the road with their dolls and toys. She then accelerated? I was transfixed and gripped on to the sides of the leather bucket seat. I thought they are dead! But she must have had an arrangement with these kids for she kept in a straight line and the kids all rolled backwards to both sides of the road at the last split second, it was hair-raising.

Charles and Ruth's daughter, Carol Saunders-White served in the USA Peace Corps for two years in Belize, Central America. Her assignment was to help the local women create local Arts and Crafts. I do not know what became of her after this. They came to England the following year. That was the first and last time my mother and he had spent time together for 64 years.

I then went to Florida. When I landed I really thought that I had landed in Mexico. Everyone spoke Spanish. Next morning I went to a garage and said I wanted to hire a big car. I had already purchased I big Stetson hat for the occasion. When the owner brought it round I was shocked by its size. It was an open top big White Cadillac. I wanted to experience one of these big cars because I knew that they would soon be too expensive to run. I had owned a Rolls Royce, a James Young Silver Cloud 2 until someone offered me a lot of money for it. I think it went to the USA. The Registration was SCT 100, which was the design number.

I drove off towards Naples, on the West coast I think it is the 41. It was a two lane road without central division. There were no other cars on the road which suited me, for I wanted to see if I could spin this car with a handbrake turn. I had seen it in so many American movies. On my first attempt I only got a quarter turn, second attempt about half way. Third attempt again about the same, I will have to try harder, faster. Suddenly a young man stood up from sitting in the grass verge, "What are you doing?" he asked, I told him. "Do you realize that there are crocodiles either side in these everglades and they will get you if you slide into the water" "OH." I replied. I asked him what he was doing, and found that he wanted to get to Naples so we went to Naples together and deprived the crocodiles of a tasty sunburnt Englishman

SICK AS A DOG

She got bad sunstroke
But could have avoided that
For the sake of a hat!

Senryu.

NORMANS ABNORMALITY (Adult poem)

Oh dear my thing is bent, it leans to the left
I think it is broken, it is severely bent
I am useless, unless I meet a girl
that has got a left hand thread
Or is it to the right, I do not know
Then I heard the tailor ask, Sir,
which way, which side, do you dress
and realised that I was normal
Well as normal as I could be
So Norman feeling his enormity
as was his normal activity
went happily on his way
knowing he could after all
possibly have his naughty way.

PROSPERITY

Private, policed, protected palisades of
portentous palaces with pillared porticoes where
motionless magnificent Mercedes motors make the
picture perfect polished perception of prosperity.

Servants silently slave serving superb servings of
delightful, decorative delicious dishes designed to
tastefully tempt to tickle taste-buds totally, till
falling faint feeling full, fasting followed until

The minute masseuse massages, manipulating
muscles. Painfully pressing pressure points
persistently teasingly tortured till tiny tears trickle,
"TONG", I cry. (Pain) An area of Kuala-Lumpar,
Malaysia.

MY MOTHER. (Adult poem)

Alice Irene Green, me marvellous mother
Nee Saunders-White. She was interesting
and captivating like no other

Loving, loyal, amusing and very strong
She paddled me bum with a brush
a wooden hairbrush, when I did wrong

Dad, Alfred Edwin Green, a male chauvinist
Liked to be seen, as a hard tough man
Cold, no cuddles never saw him kiss or be kissed.

When aged ten, I walked into a room
To find, him and Mum were fighting
Both of them grasping the handle of a broom

Face to face, swaying to the left and right
It was an even match, until mothers
sharp kick to his goolies ended this fight.

IMMIGRATION

People in poverty
due to global warming
Which way? North is best

Senryu. Note. Desert sands are expanding.

ILLUSION, DELUSION. (Adult poem)

We walked into the wilderness
Sandy soil, scrub and birch trees
The heather was deep and soft
inviting us to lie down, a soft bed
The darkness closed around us
like a velvet protective cloak

The silence was unusual
as if the darkness muffled all sound
Alone in the darkness, no moon
just the tops of the hills visible
We lay there carefree kissing cuddling
undressing each other carefully, slowly

Warmth of our bodies defied the chill
as we merged into one with each other
I was lost in a crescendo of passion as
she cried out as if in pain as she moved
I knew she was in erotic ecstasy, then
there was a sudden roaring in my ears

It was a military tank moving towards us
but we were in heaven on earth
I not want to move. We will not and we will
become a melange crushed together forever
The engine stopped. We stood up
"I was laid on a wood-ants nest", she said.

Soldiers rose like living dead from fox-holes.
We were in the middle of Army manoeuvres.

MACKEREL FISHING – (Adult story)

It was in the late 1960's and my wife Ann and I had divorced. I was living in the back room of Alf's Café and our two children were living with their mother just down the road at Wilmslow. I was still interested in parachuting despite the injuries that I had suffered and attended a meeting in Devon, which I have always adored for its wonderful rocky countryside with numerous clean rivers tumbling down the valleys.

I had put a mattress in the back of my Green Bedford van to sleep in, it was very comfortable but I had no cooking facilities. The weather caused the event to be cancelled and one of the parachutists showed me a delightful fishing village on the North coast. The village was set at the bottom of high cliffs that form a half-circle around the bay, there were some fishing boats that had been hauled up the beach.

We had lunch in one of the many small establishments that line the seafront and where I met local people that were interested in parachuting. After lunch my colleague had to go, so the lady of the house escorted me on a walk along the front. It is not a fishing village but the boats are mostly to take out paying fishing enthusiasts. Apparently the family that I was having lunch with; went fishing for one of the fishmongers in the village. During lunch I remember that I was told that there was a large telescope on the roof of their house for watching the ships.

When she and her husband found out that I was sleeping in the van I was invited to stay at their house. I slept very well, and awoke to find the wife, Susan sitting on the side of the bed, it was about 5am and she had made me a cup of tea. We talked and when she put her hand on me it became apparent that she wanted a closer relationship. She and I arranged to go out sightseeing next day which was a Sunday. I had the Monday off because it was a bank holiday. Her husband went to play golf.

We spent the whole afternoon on top of the cliffs overlooking the picturesque village in the distance below. The sun was shining and we spent a lot of time in the van and picnicked on the hilltop bench while watching the boats sailing in the bay.

That evening there was a dinner with family and friends at a restaurant, I noticed a frosty exchange of words during the meal but it did not appear to involve me. Before the meal ended I was invited by Susan's husband to go mackerel fishing next morning, I readily agreed and in the morning the three of us assembled on the beach, Susan's husband his father in law and my-self. The sea was calm with a strong swell. The boat was a beautiful craft about 20ft long and made of mahogany, It was clinker built and riveted together with copper rivets and varnished to a very high standard. An outboard motor was fitted to the transom.

The atmosphere was jovial as we pulled the boat off the beach and set off. None of us had life jackets and there was no flotation equipment on the boat. The father in law was operating the outboard motor and hubby was sitting beside him. I was facing them sitting in the centre as we left the beach. I had assumed that we would be using fishing rods to catch the mackerel but they explained that they were fishing mackerel for the local shop so they used a Long line system, They pointed out the line which was a nylon rope about 200 metres long with enormous fishhooks of about 6cm long attached at approximately one metre intervals. I had expected that bait would be used but on each hook were coloured feathers which they said were irresistible to mackerel. At one end was a huge weight with 28lbs stamped on it, I had seen these type of weights used in coal merchants.

We were now getting quite a long way out to sea when I noticed that they had stopped talking to me and each other. They were looking at each other with meaningful glances and their body language showed tension. Truly the atmosphere had become icy. I then thought, 'Oh bloody hell the telescope on the roof' and it is most likely that we had been seen on the cliff top.

I also realized that they would throw the weight over the side while at speed so the rope and hooks would unwind quickly from its position coiled beside me. It would be easy for those hooks catch on my clothing and I would be pulled over the side and it would be impossible to extricate my-self from those hooks. I moved backwards to sit on the prow of the boat away from those hooks and kept my eyes on them.

They never spoke but their looks could kill. I sat there perched on the prow, silent and impassive. I thought they were probably reluctant to start a fight with me for three reasons. Parachutists have a reputation for being fighters. It would not be good at an inquest if I had bruises or injuries and it was possible we could be seen fighting from the shore.

But this is all conjecture and the ramblings of a guilty mind. They then decided for some reason not to fish and returned to shore in silence where I jumped off without speaking and left them to haul the boat up the beach. I went to the house and told Susan I was leaving but did not tell her what had transpired.

As I was getting into the van her husband came running around the corner towards me. I thought that he wanted a fight and I stepped out to confront him but I was astonished when he held out his hand. I took his hand and it was a handshake but no words were spoken by either of us. I then got into the van and drove away pondering on the puzzle.

Was the handshake an apology for considering getting rid of me or was it just that I was leaving? I will never know.

JUNK ART

There is a sickness
if a dirty bed is art
the art world is mad.

Haiku.

Note. The artist is just taking advantage of
a stupid society.

1960's HOT & COLD. (Adult poem)

Have you ever chased
a naked lissom lady
through deep pristine snow
And felt hot blood course
your body in a burning glow
We climbed the mountain
across snow with icy crust
It was a sunny winter day
We were on a slippery slope
both with an intent to play

I chose a very peaceful spot
She was hot, snow so cold
We were not too young or old
Was it love? Perhaps just lust
I will just let the story unfold
We were both bare, without a care
She lay beneath me, loving me?
On the deep icy cold snow
She did not complain or cry
I never asked, I will never know

For every action, there is a reaction
And here was no exception
As we started to play
With arms outstretched she slid
off downhill, very quickly away
She looked like a shooting star
as she cried out; Au revoir
Where she went, nobody knows
Leaving me with just a memory
and a bag of her 1960s clothes.

HUMOUR. (Adult poem)

I was told that in far off Kazakhstan
there were three women to every man

So I thought I'd take a holiday there
and see if there was any going spare

Then I was told that some are not such nice ladies
Catch you, by getting pregnant for maintenance fees

I've seen on late TV, naked ladies of different races
holding phones and pulling the most peculiar faces?

So I decided to keep my money in the bank
watch that naughty television and have a walk.

Note. This is mainly manly fun and mickey taking.
A friend of mine is working in far off Kasakhstan

A MORNING CHAT. (Adult poem)
A true discussion with my wife.

I'm rather delicate, virginal untouched
It's the way I was brought up, British
That is why I am so terribly ticklish

"Hah, I think you are quite mad, touched
You are worn out, used, full of rust
Before you nobody had touched my bust."

"Oh yes you say. No one, but perhaps many
had a grope of your gorgeous gorge, in hope
You'd better keep quiet, you're on a slippery slope."

CONTENTMENT

When I was a child
I desired to be older
When in peaceful valleys
I wanted to be on the hills

When on Terra Firma
I longed for the heaving sea
When caught in tumultuous ocean
I prayed for church and quiet devotion

When in sticky steamy Jungle
I wished to be in temperate lands
When obliged to drive slowly
I itched to drive faster

When watching birds
I envied their wings
When flying hot Hot-Air balloons
I completely forgot all those things.

MUMBAI. Senryu

Bombay in 1950
families slept in the street
and now, they still do

Note. Bombay was renamed Mumbai but it did not make much difference to a lot of people. In 2015 the Metro City of Mumbai had a population of 22 Million.

"THAT'S MA MAN". (Adult story)

In the 1970s my wife Ann and I separated and divorced. Fortunately it was amicable, having seen the disruption to families over divorce proceedings; it is with a certain amount of pride that the whole family are able to mix amicably.

I went on a blind date; we arranged to meet outside a pub at Staines. Her telephone voice was very Southern English more like Surrey than Hampshire. So I was surprized to find that she was Jamaican. On entering the pub I asked what she would like to drink, she asked for a sweet sherry so I ordered two.

On turning around with the drinks I found that she had gone. Obviously she did not like the look of me and had departed. I stood at the bar and drank both drinks, which has a peculiar effect on me because I normally do not drink any intoxicants. Then I saw a set of sparkling white teeth smiling at me from a dark corner of the bar. She had deliberately blended into the darkness. I soon found out that she was an actress and was full of infectious humour.

Over the next month we visited her friends, went to parties and I started staying weekends at her house which is in a very nice tree lined street in N E London. She was very talkative, entertaining and full of fun.

One day I was driving in Staines with her which was unfamiliar to me and on a junction my foot slipped of the clutch and the car shot forward into a group of Hells Angels on their treasured Harleys, it was most fortunate that I did not collide with them. They got off their bikes and surrounded the car. One came to the passenger window with his face contorted with rage, what did she do? She imitated his face, which sent all of them in convulsions of laughter. Never mind the traffic jam they caused. They started a discussion with me about my car and on departing told me that I should be more careful with my James Young, Rolls Royce Silver Cloud.

One night I was in the house when the doorbell rang, I was asked to answer the door. On opening the front door I was confronted by a huge man, his left hand shot out and grabbed my collar and lifted me off my feet. Without a word spoken he carried me down the hall with his arm outstretched. This was a tremendous display of strength as I weighed 90kg. As he passed the front room he dropped me through the open door, I stood there feeling like a baby. I heard him ask "Who is that" being described as "That," also affected my self- esteem, but being a man I did not cry.

I found her reply really funny, her reply was "That's Ma Man." He popped his head around the corner and said "Hi." I found out that he was a relative of hers and was a Taxi driver, nothing else was discussed. I was in total awe of his physique and strength and could not forget the feeling of helplessness that I had experienced.

Days went past and it was forgotten and we enjoyed days of quiet relaxation. She was studying a part in a Repertory Company and appeared in more than one Television series, she was also an excellent cook and seamstress. The garden had not been tended for many years. It could not be called a garden for there were no flowers or even grass. It was just hard packed earth trodden down by a previously owned dog.

I decided to dig it and aerate the soil. As I stood at the far end of the garden plot I observed that it was about 20 metres to the house. Behind me and on my left was a high wooden fence and to the right was a low double wire fence. Beyond this wire fence the land sloped downward past the other semi-detached houses all with identical wire fences. The fences were the only indication that these were once Council houses. Why tell you all this? I am just coming to that.

Next day was a bright and sunny Sunday, I started to dig the garden from the top end, Cups of tea and homemade cake kept coming out the back door. I was enjoying life and the physical labour, the ground was so hard I had to use a garden fork. My peace of mind was disturbed when I heard a shout of "You leave him alone." I looked up and out of the back door came a man. I recognized the dreadlocks and the multi-coloured woolly hat as belonging to a Rasta (Rastafarian.) In his right hand he held a very large knife known as a machete. He walked steadily towards me swinging the machete backwards and forwards, the sun glinting on the blade as it swung forward. With the shed behind me and the wooden fence to my left, the only escape route was downhill over those wire fences.

My brain went into overtime, I thought, I will have to hurdle over those fences but I have never hurdled. I have watched hurdlers and thought they were quite mad because they can get hurt when they screw up.

I now mentally practised my running and jumping. 'One two three four steps, jump leading with my right leg and curl my left leg up and sideways'. Oh bloody hell I cannot run away. Ah, I have a four pronged garden fork in my hands it is like a Roman Trident'. I've done fencing, not garden fencing, you know fencing with rapiers and swords.

I left the tips of the fork resting on the ground until he was in striking distance. I never spoke or showed any tension or emotion. He lifted the machete above his head to strike me. Without any conscious thought I thrust the fork at his throat and surprisingly the sharp tips went under his chin and touched the skin of his neck.

My Army fencing master of many years ago would have been very proud of me. He froze and we remained in a silent statuesque state for what seemed like hours staring into each other's eyes. I knew what he was thinking. He was trying figure out whether I could or would; make a thrust to kill? He could not decide and slowly lowered his arm and dropped the machete, without speaking he turned and walked back into the house.

I carried on digging to release the tension in my body. A couple of minutes passed and my female friend called from the doorway. "He wants to talk to you." "Who is it?" I asked. There was a slight pause, *"It's me Uz-band."* The Surrey accent had been forgotten. "I don't wish to talk to him." "Oh please Darlin," she asked. I stepped carefully through the open doorway expecting him to attack me. He was waiting for me in the front room with a bottle of white rum and two glasses. "Have a drink with me," he said. "I don't drink," I replied. "Are you refusing to drink with me," he retorted in anger. I took the glass from his hand. He poured out two glasses then drank his glassful in one gulp. I had considered that he might poison me but as he had drunk it I copied him, I never even tasted it. He took a bunch of keys out of his pocket, handed them to me and walked out the front door.

I went to the kitchen and asked (his wife) "What is this all about?" While showing her the bunch of keys he had handed me. She said, "He has accepted you, those are the keys to this house." "Where does he live?" I asked. "Oh he lives about ten doors down the road with his Baby-love, she has had his child.

This event coupled with the fact that I had noticed she did not seem to be able to relate to my young son's needs meant that our relationship ended.

There was one final joke on her part. After I got married in 1980 my wife Peggy answered the phone and said to me that there was a lady with a cultivated English voice that wished to speak with me. The distinctive Jamaican voice said, *"Will you cum an dig ma gardin, Darlin"*.
My wife's hearing is as good as an Owl's and on hearing this she grabbed the phone and that is the end of the story.

AUTHOR

Authors work consumes
excitement leaps from pages
exhilaration

A Senryu poem by Aesthete2000

TWO ODDS MAKE IT EVEN

When I first met my Chinese wife
Phemerones made me wish to sire
she resisted my early advances
I wanted, it was self-centred desire

She crumbled under my onslaught
of attention, letters with poetic line
eventually married, but still worlds apart
although Chinese and English genes are fine

She's smart, meticulous with mathematical mind
so was confused by my scruffy style
A war of words and different worlds
left us at odds for quite a while

On my first visit to her family
to ask for consent to wed
I put my feet on her lap, for her to massage
caused concern from family, conversation dead

Being hot and humid, she went in the shower
I joined her; common sense I did lack
she, conscious of saving water, agreed
Well, I always wash her beautiful back

Two children, Wei Yeh and Kiki had watched us
by quietly laying on the floor
"Mummy, they are both in the shower,"
they cried, as they peeped under the door

She used to reproach and chide me
about being horrible and rude
now all she can complain about
is not squeezing the toothpaste tube

We have had a wonderful
thirty-six years together
It was hard going, the first three
Now combined, birds of a feather

Note. Regarding feet in the fourth verse.
The Chinese regard the feet as very dirty and should be
kept on the floor, not put on laps or tables.

BLOOD RED RAIN

Blood red cells fell from outer space
maybe marking the end of the human race
Falling in the rain from the sky
Coming from a meteorite then did multiply
Upon Sri Lanka this red rain did fall
and mystified and terrified one an all

Scientists did later find to their chuckles
the red rain looked like blood corpuscles
A meteor had hit Sri Lanka weeks earlier
It acted like an intergalactic bulk blood carrier
Chuckles faded when they studied their find
The cells divide; is it a danger to mankind?

This is a true story.

ACTING DOPEY

Alf's Café was situated on the A31 London Portsmouth road in the quiet village of Runfold in Surrey.

In the 1980's we had a bakery which supplied the café and the Milk bar that we owned in Farnham. We also had a van that delivered to the local villages. The bakery was attached to the café but had separate doors about forty metres apart. I ran the bakery single handed and started work at 4am. The café opened at 7am. One morning at about 5am two men walked into the bake house. It was not unusual to have visitors but I immediately thought these two were up to no good. I acted if I was dim, which was not hard for me to do. I smiled and greeted them with "Good morning" then continued making the bread dough. The mixer held about 112lbs of flour and when mixed I had to lift it into a wooden proving bin. They wandered around looking at everything. Then said they wanted a cup of tea and said they could do with a breakfast. "What time does the café open" they asked. "It opens at 7am, hang on I will make you a cuppa," I replied.

As I started walking to the door they came on each side of me and held my arms. I pretended it was a friendly, pally sort of act and remained relaxed and chatty as we walked in the darkness to the café door. Once inside they dashed around as I put the kettle on. "Where are the cigarettes? We are dying for a fag" they asked. "Oh they will be brought when the others arrive to open the café." I used the word 'others' to indicate a number of workers would arrive. But it would be my wife on her own, carrying the cash float and the cigarettes. It did the trick; they departed very quickly without waiting for the tea I was making.

BAKING

Elbow-deep in dough
punch out baker's rolls
dawn's warm aroma

Senryu poem by Aesthete2000

SAUSAGES

Back on the 5th May 1972, I had purchased my father's café. Known as Alf's café and was a transport driver's stop and as it was on the A31 road between London and Portsmouth it was very busy. It had a very large lorry park and could seat about fifty diners. I had previously started a coffee shop called The Milk Bar in the High street of Farnham Surrey. Between the two we were selling an enormous number of sausages in sandwiches and breakfasts. The sausages were from a national brand and were of superb quality. I was purchasing once a week and had large refrigerators to store them.]

It was sometime after 1980, I can remember because I got married that year and not long after my wife Peggy started working with me in the transport café. Incidentally it came as a great shock to her to find how hard it was after working in accounts most of her life. She now kept the café accounts, and she was very precise and kept immaculate records.

I remember it was a sunny day. We were very busy as it was lunch-time; I was in the kitchen with Violet the cook. The atmosphere was good, there was the hum of happy customers with the clink of knives and forks and clatter of the crockery from Pamela the dishwasher who made a lot of noise to prove that she was working harder than anyone else.

Suddenly I heard a clanking noise that out-clanked Pamela. It sounded as though medieval knights were advancing in their armour. I turned expecting to see a joker playing some sort of game. There were two enormous policemen advancing towards me. They were festooned with handcuffs and odd items hanging from their belts. They looked like jailers and it was the long metal extending Baton (for bashing rebellious people) that was jingling against the handcuffs. I had never seen these two policemen before, nor had I ever seen such large specimens. Later I realized why I had not seen them.

One of them grabbed my arms as if I was going to run away. He turned me to face a man in a suit that had followed in with a large entourage of people. One of them opened the fridge and identified the sausages as coming from his factory. The 120kg Policeman said "You are under arrest" and clicked the handcuffs on. Later I realized why I had not seen them. Probably not one of the local Bobbies wanted to arrest me after eating my lovely doughnuts. These big bully boys were specially selected from Reading about 30 miles away.

You see the police cars that patrolled the A31 and the local Bobbies in cars would stop by and look at the vehicles and sometimes the customers as they knew that some of our customers were characters of interest to them. I did not like them coming in the café to ask questions. So I made an arrangement with them.

I asked them to take their hats off when they came in and wait until the person they wished to speak to had finished his meal and then speak to him. The customers always went quietly. In return every policeman got a tea and one of my home made doughnuts. I think we had every policeman from Guildford, Farnham and Aldershot come in for a tea and doughnut, including my son who was a police motorcycle cop from Guildford.

They now said that I had been purchasing sausages that were stolen from their factory. I said "Don't be daft; I have been buying your sausages for over ten years." "Peg, go and get the invoices and show them." "*You have invoices?*" they all chorused in astonishment! The gorilla's grip on my wrists relaxed. Peggy went and got the invoices. After seeing the piles of company invoices that proved I had paid the proper factory price. The cuffs came off and they all went outside for a parley then disappeared without a single word of 'Sorry'. I thought at least they could have given me a few sausages.

On the next delivery of their sausages, the new driver told me that there had been two production lines in the factory for over ten years. Then on the delivery circuit the first delivery got a proper factory invoice. Every second customer which included me received an invoice which was printed on the same paper; by the same firm but had different numbers and the all the customers paid the full price. There was obviously a separate office for the fiddled sausages. So there were two production lines in the factory. Half of the pork and ingredients were purchased by the conspirators and half the takings were going to their pockets without the inconvenience of owning a factory, machinery, delivery vehicles or employing staff.

The driver that had been taking my sausage orders for years had the cheek to phone me and ask if I could help him out as he was married and had children.
My reply was a rather rude.

PROTECTING PLOD 05/04/2013

To avoid a Police Health and Safety insurance claim
When burglars burgle your business or home
If you have to call the Plod, make it your aim
If you let the police enter you establishment
Be it freehold or a leasehold property
It seems you must first make a full risk assessment
Before Plod enters make sure you mop the floor
of any blood, bodily fluids or grease or water for
If they slip, the lawyers will certainly make you poor
After your window or door was broken in the raid
Collect the glass and cover it or any scratch will ensure
you will be bankrupt after police compensation is paid
Then the next Insurance premium will be raised
While the criminals are rarely found or punished
The police will get gongs and officers highly praised.

Note.
A policewoman sued the owners of a garage because she tripped over something in the darkness. She would have had a torch, don't you think.

FINGER NAILS.

My transport café called Alf's on the A31 road at Runfold in Surrey was by-passed by the new road and I had to supplement my income by buying and selling old furniture. I named it the Junk Shop at first but soon changed it to Runfold Antiques. It was the same stuff I sold but people do not like their furniture described as junk. I was buying newly constructed pine furniture and treating it with acid to make it look older, it also gave it a very nice colour and shading. I did tell purchasers if it was not old.

One day I was finishing the process with a coating of wax on a table when a young man came in to see me. He had grown up in the village and frequented the café very often. He had come to ask me a question, I cannot remember what it was but as I pondered on the reply I put my fingers to my cheek. Immediately there was a look of horror on his face and he ran out of the shop. I had no idea what his problem was, I carried on polishing.

A few minutes later his father came crashing through the door. Crashing is an apt description because he is built like a Brick-S***-house (shed) or like a Bulldozer. His eyes were blazing with anger. "What are you playing at?" He shouted. I looked at him with a puzzled look as I had no idea what he was on about. He grabbed my wrists and pulled my arms towards him.

This was a person that you did not mess around with, for his strength was renowned. He was a bare fist fighter. If you have never heard of this I will explain. The two fighters place their bets with the referee and then fight, the one left standing collects the money. His favourite trick was to grab his opponent by the neck with one hand and lift him off the ground which would immobilize them and then he could pulverize them with the other fist.

His hands were easily twice the size of mine. He turned my hands around and shoved my finger nails in front of my bewildered eyes. My nails were the most amazing brown colour. They looked as though I had painted and varnished them, ladies pay twenty five quid or more for nails to look like that.

I very quickly told him that it was the result of the acid that I was using. "Oh, thank God for that he said. My son thought that you had gone Gay".

It was the combination of what he thought were painted nails and when I pondered on his question I had placed my fingers on my cheek. This in certain circumstances and in the manner of execution can be construed as a feminine gesture. I was released from the vice-like grip and given a pardon.

MESSERSMIT

Swanage town centre
Seagulls dive-bombed people
eating fish-n-chips

Senryu

INFORMATION

All Leaders, past, present ,new and old
having gained control of a country's wealth
ensure their pockets are lined with gold

Misinformation is the key
fed by television and radio
to the likes of you and me

Hitler mastered films, for propaganda
combined with radio transmissions
everyone suffered from his megalomania

T.V. and radio then came into play
like scenes from Orwell's, "Nineteen eighty four"
now it seems to have had its day.

Note. George Orwell's story 1984 is with us now.

THE GREEN WOMAN

I am turning Green
You're wearing a silk dress
Reflecting sunlight!

Senryu.

A true story. This lady came to me with a genuine concern! Her face had an interesting green sheen.

Senryu poem.

THE FUNNY FARM

In the 1980's I owned a James Young Silver Cloud Rolls-Royce (Design Number SCT 100). It was a most beautiful aluminium bodied handmade car. It had a division made of burr walnut complete with a cocktail cabinet with cut glass and silver items. It cost me £2,500in the1970s. I was fortunate to find a scooter with the registration number SCT 100 which I put on this car. I had purchased this car as a gift to my father in the 1970's but he sold it to my brother's company. My brother did not want it so I re-purchased it from him at a cost of £3,000. It was the best investment I ever had. When I sold it I think it went to America.

I was very keen to know everything about this car and joined the Rolls Royce Owners Club and collected all the back issues of their magazine. I was missing about five of the old back issues and placed an advert for them. I had a reply from North Yorkshire from a farmer that said I could call on him to discuss the magazines that I required. One day after finishing my baking in the cafe I set off to see him and arrived in the remote village in the late afternoon.

This was the days before the use of the Sat-Nav and when I stopped at the local village and asked a woman where the farm was. She gave me a funny look and just walked away, I thought it was because she thought I was foreigner or perhaps just because I was a Southerner. I then asked a young couple, and they said "You don't want to go up there; do you? I said I was invited, so the man gave me directions, "Out of the village and up the hill."

By now it was now pitch dark as I drove down an unmade private road and into the farmyard. There was only one dim light coming through the small glass window in the door set in a range of low buildings that were dimly silhouetted against the sky. I got out of the car and walked through thick mud to get to the door and knocked with the large brass door knocker. After some time a man opened the door, he looked very surprised to see me and demanded, "Who are you?" I told him I was Mr Green about the Rolls Royce Magazines. "How did you get here?" he asked. "By car," I replied. "Where's the car? "Over there," I said and pointed into the darkness in the general direction.

"Oh you had better come in." he said as he turned and led me down a dark narrow corridor only lit by a dim light coming from a doorway. I thought that I was in the cows milking parlour because of the muddy state it was in until I looked into a room as I passed. It was a kitchen. There were empty food tins piled and empty milk bottles covering the tables and the floor, Dirty pots pans and plates spilled over from the sink.

I followed my host into the room at the end of the corridor. It was an extremely large room; like a barn with a huge log fire burning a pile of three foot long oak logs. There were two large high backed chairs facing the fire. All around the sides of the room were shelves of books, and magazines. On the floor stacked very neatly up to the ceiling were old newspapers all carefully folded and in separate files according to the title and in date order. Then I saw the Rolls Royce magazines, all in pristine condition on their respective shelves in date order.

At that moment I saw a movement in one of the chairs, I had not seen the old woman sitting there. "Go and make tea." The man of the house ordered.

She rose very slowly and I could see her shape left in the chair. As she shuffled away I could see she had an extraordinary amount of clothes on. Both her legs were bound in filthy crepe bandages; the ends of which were trailing along the floor behind her. She looked like an Egyptian Mummy! Thinking about the state of the kitchen I declined the tea that I was offered. I realized that neither of them undressed and sat and slept in those two high backed chairs beside the fire.

He asked me what issues of the magazine I wanted. As He picked out the five I wanted from the rack, I found out she was not a mummy as the farmer told me they had never had children. I asked how much he wanted for them and he replied that they were a gift as he had no dependents to leave them to. We had a short chat about my car; as the mummy shuffled back to the chair without making any tea at all and fell back with a woomf noise into the cushions and blankets. These had a permanent impression of her body shape.
Then he said, "Come and see mine."

As we stepped out of the door that I had entered he warned me, "Stay exactly behind me as there are traps for unwanted visitors." As we passed my Jaguar car I saw in his torchlight that he had left the lids off of the cesspits! I had unknowingly walked in between the open cesspits. Had I gone down into those deep tanks I certainly would not have lived as the gasses will kill in minutes and nobody knew I was visiting this farm.

In an open barn was a beautiful old Rolls Royce of the type that had a division between the driver and his passengers. The coachwork was reminiscent of the horse carriage era. I did not ask questions for I was preoccupied with the thought of getting out of the premises safely. He opened the bonnet and there was a pristine example of the engineering that made the car famous. He then shone the torch into the back of the car, where I had expected to see grey padded upholstery with silk tassels and speaker tube to speak to the chauffeur. But it was full of shovels, forks, axes, saws and a wheelbarrow. The interior was covered in mud and dung. It was ruined as he used it around the farm as a general purpose vehicle. I made a comment that it was interesting that he was using it on the farm, then said that I had to go as I had a long journey.

He guided me past more than one trap with his torch and bid me goodbye. Now I understood the attitude of the locals and felt very lucky not to be at the bottom of one of his cesspit traps.

VICARIOUS

Elegant, unnecessarily precarious
She knows I'm being vicarious
Waiting, tempting, it is hilarious

Note. This poem was for a competition.
In the prompt she was standing on a chair.

THE SANDS VILLAGE

This is a story about my-self and the village
A community that worries about their image
I have lived here for over forty years
Most of it good times, with occasional tears

Two local men, new arrivals, knock on my door
That I must say does not happen any more
They did not come to shake my offered hand
but said, as they on my doorstep did stand

"To be accepted in this village, The Sands."
Now I'm thinking they are holding hands!
"You should drink at our pub, The Barley Mow
or join the Golf club, it is rather nice, you know."

I replied that I was teetotal, I did not drink
Broke my spine skydiving, golf won't help I think
Others had said; "You should not be in this place."
This was said with a deadpan, serious face

"This village is for airline pilots, doctors, dentists
I admit this made me mad and clench my fists
I said, there are too many dentists, I expect
Pilots are like taxi drivers now, doctors I respect

Aircraft, now like drones can do without pilots
I have owned two aircraft, I advise these idiots
Probably with mortgages and small backyards
Company cars and living on their credit cards?

I've not been cheated by a working man or gypsy
If you are honest they treat you respectfully
Café's food given on credit, payment never missed
Local business men have cheated me, I have a list

Locals dumped garden waste in my pristine wood
They would dump all their trash if they could
I let them walk their dogs in my garden property
They would not keep them under control properly

That group said, "You don't like dogs, do you?"
I said "I prefer children not to be covered in poo."
They think I am an impecunious lunatic, I'm sure
I said F-off, I never said that to them before,

I have all the T shirts. Have done it all
Merchant Navy, Air Force, Army, Pilot, Free-fall
Owned motorbikes, Rolls Royce and Yacht
Two aircraft, five Hot air balloons, that's a lot

British Skydiving School, two café's, a quarry
A bit naughty with ladies, caused lots of worry
While engaged in all this work, fun and games
been cursed, cussed, accused given bad names

There is a problem, many people view success
with envy, jealousy and try to get you in a mess
Married twice, English Ann, three kids, that's nice
Over thirty years with Chinese Peggy, lots of rice

As 'Simpleton', I've written about people I've met
Told in stories on Allpoetry.com on the internet
Eaten lots of salt, that means coped with strife
Suffered many fools, but we have enjoyed our life.

I KILLED A SPIDER

A spider came into my view, my vision
as I watched the news on television
I clapped my hands without thinking
and killed this harmless little thing

Then I thought, I should have stopped
taken him to the window and dropped
Then he would have sailed away
on a thread to live another day

I then watched another spin his web
who put the knowledge in his head?
How to spin, to cast adrift on a thread
Is it in the genes, taught or inbred

Tigers, Gorillas, Rhino's I wish to preserve
but spiders, also have a right and deserve
to live, and as they catch irritating flies
which help to improve and protect our lives.

A WAIL

Befriend a whale
The Japanese will thank you
Easier to harpoon.

The Japanese are killing whales. Why? It's profit.
They pretend it is for research but plenty of
whales are dying on the beaches probably due
to military sonar type noises. They could all be
examined. They are probably making pet food,
getting oils and making perfume from ambergris.

BALLOONING STORIES

DASHING DAVID

David. C. Johnson apparently liked moving fast. But I was unaware of this tendency. I had the good fortune to meet him through my interest in Hot Air Ballooning. He was and is a highly qualified Aviation expert and was a balloon pilot. He owned a balloon but it is interesting to fly other types and different manufacturer's balloons.

I had only flown eight times as a passenger when I had the opportunity of purchasing a balloon that had only flown five hours flying time. The owner lived in London and had found it too difficult to organize his retrieve crew and get out into the country to fly. It was as new, an absolute bargain but I had to have a qualified pilot to accompany and teach me until I qualified.

It was on the 24th of April 1988. Crikey! That was twenty-five years ago but it seems like only last week that we got together at Tony Browns place at Worplesdon, Guildford. Tony was a commercial balloon pilot and examiner. He checked the balloon for any faults or damage, there was none. It was an AX 77 Registration number G-BNHS we nicknamed it 'Nursey'. It was a very pleasant yellow, red, and white colour and could carry three people comfortably.

But this flight was for my training so there was just David and myself. We took off at 7.30 am. Early starts are the norm to avoid the thermic activity that glider pilots love and look for. The wind speed was slow at first and we travelled at a leisurely pace over Aldershot, Church Crookham, past Odiham to Hook then we started to speed up as we tracked towards Basingstoke down the M3. I must admit that it is boring to be in a balloon that is only traveling at a walking pace.

David was obviously in his element. We were directly over the M3 motorway and now it seemed that we were held in this corridor of wind, and it got faster. Then I noticed that we were travelling as fast as the cars down on the M3.

I said "David, we are going as fast as the cars on the motorway!" "Yeerse," he replied, then said "We are going to need a very large field." He said this laconically with no sign of emotion. There were large fields either side of the motorway but the wind was enjoying the freedom of the highway. Then David commented that the road bore off to the left at the junction leading into Basingstoke. But that still meant getting across the sprawling great town and we were getting low on our propane gas.

I recalled and told David that there was a park this side of the intersection called Black Dam and this was directly in our path as the road bent off slightly southwards. David took over he controls and flew as low as he could over the traffic.

The park I now know is called Crab Tree Park and the East end of it is on a low hill with the park sloping down to a fishpond at the intersection. We came over some trees and David pulled on the Parachute cord which opens the top of the balloon and lets the hot air out. Then he shut off the burners just before we hit the turf surface. It seemed we had a mile of grass in front of us as the balloon envelope collapsed and the basket tipped onto the side causing David's bulky form to squash me as the wind continued to pull us down the slope on damp grass. We hurtled along bumping up and down as we both closed the valves on the propane tanks. There were some people in the park but they quickly got out of the way as we shouted to them and eventually slowed and stopped at the bottom of the park just before the path and the fish pond.

As we climbed out of the basket a police car came rocketing through the gate and pulled up beside us. "Are you OK?" They asked, "We saw you above us on the motorway and thought you were in serious trouble!" David thanked them for their concern and told them it was a bit fast but we were alright.

It was not long before the retrieve vehicle and crew turned up and followed the police into the park which made the packing up easy. We had dragged and bumped approximately 500 metres. It could have been quite different trying to land safely in the middle of Basingstoke.

Note. I am constantly reminded of David by the space ranger cartoon character Buzz Lightyear. It is the way that Buzz takes every difficult situation in a cool and calm manner.

Don't tell him I think he looks like Buzz Lightyear.

A NICE FRIGHT

This is a story about a hot-air balloon flight and a ramble through my mind. As a child I loved to ramble across the countryside and even in local estates and large gardens. It was an insatiable curiosity that I had, and yet my teachers called me bird-brain and my mother said I was scatter-brained.

It was a hot sunny day in 1946 when at East Street School in Farnham Surry. I was twelve years old and in Mr Howells class. He was the one that used to punch me on the head. He punched most of the boys if they got something wrong and cuddled the girls while explaining to them in detail their errors.

I was day dreaming as usual about being out in the countryside when I wondered whether I would be alive in the year 2000 and if I was, what would I be doing? No amount of childish imagination could conjure up the life that I have enjoyed. Flying a Hot Air balloon satisfied all my longing to explore. Not only was I still alive beyond the year 2000 but I had obtained a commercial balloon licence to fly Hot-Air balloons.

This story is about a terrible fright, and it was on my First Solo Flight.it was a beautiful day any day when you can fly is wonderful. Not wet, not too windy, or too hot. Hot means you cannot lift so much and you can melt the balloon nylon. Hot sun also means thermals which will lift and throw your balloon up and down all over the sky. You do want some wind because it is really boring to stand still in the sky. If I messed up on this flight I would not have got my licence.

We assembled in a park called Shalford Green on the South side of Guildford in Surrey on the 14th July 1991. My balloon by then was a size 0-84 Registration G-BROS which I had purchased new in April 1990.

The wind was steady but fast, 20 mph straight over the town. This meant a fast take-off to clear the nearby Guildford houses on a hill in front of us. An added problem was that I had to stay airborne for 30 minutes to pass the test. That would be fine anywhere else but the wind was going directly to London Heathrow Airport which was less than thirty miles away. I commented on this point to my examiner to which all he replied was "Observe."

There were other experienced balloonists there that wanted to hop over Guildford. As they prepared to take off, my son Bernie who was a policeman in this area arrived on his Police motor-bike. "Dad," he implored. "Don't take off in this wind."

We watched as an old hand prepared to take off. He was alone in his basket as he did not wish to risk taking a passenger although he had room for three persons. His balloon retaining strop was taut, tied to a Land Rover. It was straining and creaking to break away. He pulled the metal quick release buckle which promptly flew back and hit his head knocking him out cold. He fell into the basket out of sight. The balloon flew off slowly gaining height but with no heat input it faltered and started sinking towards the centre of Guildford. There was nothing that could be done except watch. Just before it was about to crash into the chimney pots, a head and hand appeared and reached for the burners, they lit up and it climbed away.

My son Bernie pleaded with me again not to go but I saw it as the only way to prove my ability. I had observed that the upper clouds were not moving so if I climbed quickly I might be able to remain airborne for the required half hour despite the close proximity of Heathrow. There was a distinct antipathy towards new balloon pilots in those days by the 'In-crowd' because it was like a closed shop; they would like me to fail.

I had a soft silky retaining rope which gave me a trouble free take-off. I climbed as fast as I could but had time to look at the Cathedral. My name is on one of its bricks, which I think I paid half a crown for in 1946. That was one eighth of an English pound. It is built entirely of reddish bricks, a bit ugly by most standards but you must visit it if you are passing by as it has a certain charm and it is on a hill overlooking Guildford.

The higher I went the slower the wind blew and looking down I had come almost to a stop. I relaxed and opened a tin of soft drink, then looked to the South East and the following balloons, then towards the East down the length of the Hog's Back which is a six mile ridge of chalk hill going towards Farnham Surrey.

I then turned to the North East and dropped the drink can and nearly wet myself, for I was looking at the big wheels and undercarriage of a Jumbo-Jet. I could see the rows of rivets in the aluminium fuselage; it was that close. I reached up and pulled out the top of the balloon which is like a parachute held in place by the hot air. The balloon responded by dropping like a stone as the jet with its four screaming engines passed directly overhead. The balloon envelope shook or was it my legs causing the shaking? With the planes angle of climb for take-off, the pilots could not see the balloon as I was directly in front of them. Nor do balloons show up on Radar very well.

I was now in the fast lower wind and time was now my enemy. Now there were fields below, the wind slows a little by friction with the trees and the earth. So I skimmed inches above the fields. A deer stood up and ran before me ducking through a hedge, and then he stood still thinking he had evaded me but I popped over the hedge to follow him again until he veered away. I knew the following balloons would time my landing and I waited till the last field near Effingham Junction adjoining the M25 Ring road around London before landing those last precious inches below the basket. I had flown 35 minutes and travelled over ten miles.

I now had my wings for Hot Air Balloons; I do wish I had taken up ballooning earlier but Gas ballooning was terribly expensive and it was only the creation of the propane burner and the nylon hot air balloon that made it feasible for me to take part in such a wonderful pastime, although the cost of a balloon was equivalent to a decent family car and running costs were roughly £100 per hour including the retrieve vehicle costs.

Unfortunately when the large commercial balloons started carrying 12 to 16 people the Farmers decided they should charge landing fees of £100 plus. The farmers could not tell the difference between a commercial flight and a family or friends on a pleasure flight and it ended up with a lot of unpleasant arguments. I have had Firework rockets fired at the balloon. Land-rovers driven at the basket as I landed even fisticuffs and plenty of bad language some of that through loudspeakers. Not very nice for their neighbours and it upsets animals.

One lady owner released her horses from the stables in the hope they would frighten me and trample on the balloon fabric but that but that did not work as the horses nuzzled me, so she said I must be a nice person and opened the gates to let us get out of the high fenced field. The nastiest trick was a small landowner that ran his tractor over my friend's balloon. Ballooning satisfied all my cravings for excitement, fun and flight, I do miss it now I am too old to be a Commercial Hot-Air Balloon Pilot. I still like a fast ride on my 600cc Honda.

TIME

Sitting in school, time stood still
Eight hours of boring work my fill
Time always drags in a queue
There are times, time flies for you
You are driving a car, half awake
You see an accident, you brake
Time slows, when your life to preserve
Seeing vehicle positions, people to observe
Their faces, their places, the cause the cat
Crunch, slow motion impact, things like that
Time is governed by our brains reaction
While it works out a defensive action.

A FLYING BRICK

Dave Johnson's, Hot Air Balloon was capable of carrying two people. It would have carried three when new but it was a few years old now. The colour was an attractive yellow which enabled it to be seen easily when it has landed. Also as it was relatively small and light it was easy to pack up.

One day in the early 1990's Dave suggested we swop balloons for the next flight which would take us over the Town of Farnham in Surrey. My balloon was new and had two Burners, meaning it had two little propane burners as engines which individually could throw out a fifteen foot intense flame into the Balloon envelope. Under normal conditions the pilot only used one burner. When changing to a full propane tank after exhausting the previous tank, you could fly the balloon on the second burner which was connected to a third tank.

An important point was that if you had burner failure which is the same as engine failure you could fly on the second burner. Dave's balloon only had one burner. In the basket was always a mechanical flint lighter to relight the burner if it went out. And they could and did blow out occasionally.

I owned a balloon but I had not obtained my pilot's licence so I was accompanied by a lady pilot called Lulu. We took off South of Farnham and our track was over the town and towards Aldershot, on rising to 1500ft I found that we were veering towards Farnborough in Hampshire. David had taken off some way behind us.
But I did not even look at him once for the simple reason, his balloon flew like a brick compared to my new one which floated along. The Rip-stop material of

155

the Balloon envelope becomes more porous with time and the degradation of the sun's rays and the heat from the burning propane. In my balloon I could burn for a couple of seconds and relax; look around at the view, take photos.

But in Dave's balloon I could not relax for a second it seemed as soon as you stopped burning we started dropping out of the sky like a brick.

Heating up the balloon and take off, uses a lot of propane and I realized that we would be over Farnham when the first tank would be empty and I would have to change to the next full propane tank. This would mean that the burner would be out of gas while I changed over and reignited the gas. I did not fancy the idea of dropping like a brick into Farnham town.

Not thinking to tell Lulu of my intentions, I decided to practice reigniting the propane burner while we were over fairly large country gardens. I gained some height, about 2000ft and with the flint lighter in my right hand turned the burner completely off.

Lulu's reaction took me by surprize, She started punching and slapping me. She thought I'd gone mad until I had relit the flame and quickly explained my purpose. I explained that we would drop out of the sky when we transferred to the second tank. I did not wish to be over the town when that happened; so I wanted to practice and be ready and prepared.

Now I realized that we were heading towards Farnham Park, we could land there but Sod's law prevailed and all the way we had Power lines, trees roads or houses in the way. We changed tanks in military precision. Now we were fast approaching Upper Hale with dense housing estates and behind that was a fresh water conservancy area in which it was prohibited to enter. But worse still directly beyond that was the famous Farnborough Airfield.

On top of the hill in front of us I saw a patch of grass behind a low wooden shed on the opposite side of the Upper Hale road, the A3016. On the south side the hillside is covered with private housing. On the North side there is a huge housing estate called Sandy Hill Estate and to the West of the entrance was this Boy Scout hut with a grass area of only about 60ft by 100ft. I was terrified of going into prohibited airspace, there were penalties. I never had a radio to call up the control tower and tell them where I was heading. I knew that Balloons do not show up on radar. I was determined to land on that equivalent of a postage stamp.

The problem with flying over a hill is that the prevailing wind is compressed by the hill and speeds up. We were travelling quite fast now. We skimmed over the houses and just before the road we went between the chimney pots. It is a good job there was not a high lorry or furniture van in the way as we crossed the road. Down over Scout hut at the same angle as the incline of the felt roof and wallop onto the grass. Normally a landing like that would mean a bounce. The Brick did not bounce!

As the envelope quickly collapsed a Police Panda car drove into the compound. This was not a car shaped like a Panda but a local low powered police car, for some reason, perhaps due to the paintwork the public nicknamed it 'A Panda Car.' A Male Sergeant and a policewoman jumped out and he started giving me a lot of verbal.

The Sergeant said he was going to report me to the aviation authorities for numerous supposed offences.
I explained I could not land earlier because of housing, power lines etc. "Then why have you landed in a housing area? You could have landed further on" he said. When I told him there was a water conservancy ahead, he said "Rubbish" He obviously was not a local man.

While this was going on a collection of about twenty children; mostly boys of about ten to twelve years of age were gathering behind the police. At this moment I was gently pushed aside by Lulu, who then introduced herself to the Sergeant in the cultivated voice of someone used to mixing in high society.

At this precise moment a young boy caught my attention by holding up two half bricks in his hands and by nodding and flicking his eyes at the police. This little boy was asking me if I wanted him to throw them at the police. At the same moment I saw that all the children were carrying stones or half-bricks. Although feeling rather peeved at the policeman I shook my head. At this all of the children were definitely disappointed, but I not only was thinking of the welfare of the police but I did not want David's balloon damaged by flying bricks although I had designated it as a Flying Brick.

Diplomacy worked, Lulu's charm worked a treat the police beat a retreat without a barrage of bricks. I had not listened to her conversation and I doubt that her connections with the Lord High Sherriff and Police had anything to do with the eventual pleasant ending to our eventful flight.

FRESH AIR

Look miserable
Spray from can then look happy
Do not breathe the spray

Senryu

Note, Read the warning on the tin
On the 22/02/16. There was an article by Sean Poulter
on how air fresheners could be killing you.

WIND

Soft bodied people
must always hide underground
when hurricanes come

Haiku.

ALICE'S 80ᵀᴴ BIRTHDAY

I gave my mother a ride in my big balloon
brushed the branches of a springy birch
Travelled through the Devils Punchbowl valley
and passed between the spires of a church

Stopped still, sitting like a seagull
on the top branches of a tall beech
The village cricketers stopped to shout
We'll send for help, our ladders won't reach

We let them run around and fret a while then
My mother shouts, "do not worry we're alright"
I had to allay their fears, and told them, we
stopped to watch you. We'll continue our flight

We climbed to view the wooded countryside
and felt the damp kiss of cumulous cloud
and being high up there feeling close to god
felt un-willing to re-join the earthbound crowd

Approached to land at a country mansion
in the beautiful Surrey village of Fernhurst
Ended up landing on a big house front lawn
Her Ladyship invited us to tea, to slake our thirst

In the front lounge of this large house
we sat and laughed as the table was laid
for my mother spoke and entertained, as
they talked of her days as an under-stairs maid.

Note. This is a true account of a memorable Hot Air balloon flight. My mother was sold into service with a family in London when she was only twelve years of age. Within two years she had contracted TB. (Tuberculosis) and spent two years in a Sanatorium in Kent 1916-1918. In 1987 when my son became a policeman I took my mother to his passing out parade at the Police Academy in Ashford Kent. As we sat there with the band playing and the police parading past my mother suddenly went for a walk. She had realized that the wooden huts that were on this site had been the TB sanatorium that she lived in 69 years before and that within the month they were to be pulled down, an amazing coincidence. She was able to enter the very hut that she had lived in and which was being demolished within that month.

RELAX

If you can't relax
or are unable to sleep
Just twiddle your toes.

Note. The brain cannot be anxious
and twiddle toes at the same time.

Haiku.

AGE

Eighty is not fun
Being Ninety must be worse
is there an age pill?

Senryu

THE POT OF GOLD

On the fifth January 1994
With my friend Geoff Boyes
Flying a Hot Air Balloon together
In sunny but showery weather
I burn gas, phsst-phsst, and climb
The sun behind us begins to shine

Cumulous clouds around us
Rain made the hot balloon heavy
A dark balloon in front of us did show
It's our shadow surrounded, and aglow
by a complete circular bright rainbow
shining on the puffy white cloud below.

I always wanted to be in the sky
Now you might wonder why
As a child I was often told
There was a pot of gold
At the end of the rainbow
How I found it, I'll tell you so

You already have it, it is life
Although often you will suffer strife
The pot of gold is with you and me
The ability to feel, walk, talk and see
To be able to think and just to be
It is the gift of life, given to us for free

Note.
The image of my balloon on the cloud in front of us with a complete circular very bright rainbow in a ring around our shadow was a most beautiful sight and I think is rarely seen.

162

1989 FRENCH BALLOON FESTIVAL.

My son Marc and I competed in the FRATERNITE BALLOON FESTIVAL at Metz in northern France during 28th July to 6th of August 1989. It was the Bicentenary of the French Revolution. I wonder what those revolting revolutionaries would think of all those rich capitalists cavorting in their expensive colourful air carriages which did not carry goods or take travellers to specific destinations but fairly aimlessly wander across the skies.

This was the largest assembly of Balloons ever to take place. Laid across the immense airfield were rows of car tyres about fifty metres apart. We were issued with a number which indicated where we to lay out our balloons ready for take-off. I was in the second row which pleased me because there were many hundreds of balloons and I prefer to lead not follow.

On finding the tyre with our number painted on it Marc placed the Susuki jeep on the down-wind side. Three of us pulled the basket off the trailer and lugged it to the front of the jeep to attach a retaining strop to stop the balloon flying away as we prepared it for flight. As we struggled with the heavy balloon envelope in its large bag, a large white vehicle parked beside us.

It was a cross between a lorry and a Winnebago, A big ve-hic-cle. A tall well-built man got out followed by an entourage of unsmiling male nonentities. He walked slowly towards me with a rolling swagger in the manner of John Wayne. The large leather broad brimmed hat completed the desired image. He did not say Bonjour, Hallo or Hi, but said in a loud voice, "YOU ARE IN MY SPACE BUDDY." It was typical John Wayne talk,

I turned away and looked at the numbered tyre and quickly realized that there were two numbers on opposite sides of the tyre. I was on the down side of the tyre. All it meant was the balloon on the upwind side would have the top of their balloon at the tyre.

I had realized that this John Wayne lookalike was an American. He now said aggressively "WHADYA GOING TO DO BUDDY?" I replied "There is a simple solution," I bent down and turned the tyre around to face the other way. Then I said, "There you are there is your take-off slot."

I turned away to continue pulling our envelope out. He and his group stood there some time trying to grasp the situation. Then as his driver pulled the vehicle forward Big John with a theatrical flourish pressed two buttons on the side of the vehicle and with a Ka-pusch sound the back doors opened and the balloon basket came down a sliding ramp. It was might have been very impressive but there was nobody there to clap.

When all the balloons were ready, the signal was given and the first row took off followed by each row in quick succession. On gaining height of a thousand feet, I looked back and it looked like the sky was full of coloured flowers. In Northern France the terrain is flat and boring, a huge expanse of endless, treeless fields. There was a ridge on the horizon and I decided to go high to find a fast wind to reach it. Climbing at a fast rate I reached over 10,000ft. It resulted in a strange feeling of detachment from the earth far below. I know it affects passengers in another way when there is only a wicker basket under their feet and a slight swaying of the basket makes it worse. The answer is for them to grab hold of the metal handles of the propane tanks, it is strangely reassuring.

I suddenly found something in my mouth was popping and fizzing like the sherbet I used to eat as a kid. Something was in my mouth, lots of little hard bits; I spat them into my hand and discovered that it was bits of tooth? I remembered that Astronauts have to ensure there are no air pockets behind the fillings in their teeth because they will explode in the reduced air pressure at high altitude. The experience was not painful at all, just popping and fizzing and a mouthful of tiny pieces of tooth. I'd had a recent filling and the dentist had obviously left an air pocket.

We descended to 5000ft and were happily cruising along when there was a whistling and whooshing sound and a balloon came hurtling down past us with the passengers whooping and hollering at us. It was too close and dangerous for them and us. They were Americans and I think they were doing it because they were bored. When you have flat open country, it can be tedious; it is like sitting in a yacht in a dead calm sea. So to excite the passengers they collapse the balloon envelope at high altitude by opening the top parachute vent and let the hot air out, they then fall at high speed.

It is important that the pilot watches the envelope very carefully, so that it does not totally collapse into a streamer. The pilot must carefully make short hot blasts into the envelope to keep some semblance of shape and retain the ability to introduce a final blast of hot air to stop the decent. I have done it in training and in an emergency to get out of the thermal updraft of a huge cloud formation. I did get into a storm cloud once and that was seriously scary because it can carry you up to 20,000ft or more and that is deadly. British pilots are the best in the world because the UK is small and overcrowded, fields are tiny, surrounded by small forests and woods and very often fields have horses in them with very anxious owners that hate balloonists. So being able to land on a proverbial postage stamp is imperative.

As we approached the ridge I could see a town ahead and a huge number of high tension lines so I made a quick decision to land on the last farm before the ridge. Unfortunately it was quite small and had an assortment of horses, cows and pigs. In the UK farmers have on various occasions fired guns, shot firework rockets at me and screamed through megaphones to "Go away." or similar impolite words. Farm animals pick up on the vibes from humans and some sub-humans. These animals will run in all directions. Pigs are the worst; I have seen pigs run in a straight line for miles going straight through Barbed wire, electric fences and solid wooden fences. It made me realize why the hunting of wild boar was the sport of Kings and Knight's but they rode horses; but the poor peasant beaters were on foot.

I was nervous about the farmer that stood there silently watching with his family as I landed amongst the animals. I had found that if I talked to the horses as I approached to land, they would listen and not gallop away. They then understood that this monstrous bird was just another human in a horse-less carriage like a motor-car.

The French pigs kept their snouts churning up the ground. I quickly walked to the farmer and in my basic French profusely apologized for landing and gave him a bottle of best Gin. This puzzled him because he wondered why I was giving him a bottle of water.

He also asked why I was apologizing to him, that was difficult to explain so I pointed to the hundreds of balloons which I knew would also follow me to land in his farm. Our retrieve vehicle drove up so we made a fast exit because I did not want one of those balloons to land on us or my equipment and hundreds of balloons dropping in on him might not improve his happy mood.

There were other flights and the Brits were winning the competition so at lunchtime the French organizers changed the rules. They won; we were not surprized, after all we were in France.

HOT HOUSE

"Lots of things go off
in this house, milk, food," she said
I hope she doesn't

Note. Senryu

My wife told me off for leaving the milk out of the fridge

EDWARD AND LULU'S NEW BALLOON

Edward and Lulu lived in a pleasant valley on the south side of Guildford. Lulu was already an experienced hot-air balloon pilot and we had flown together many times have experienced some very unnerving moments.

They had purchased a brand new very colourful balloon. It could carry four people. Edward wanted to learn to fly it and asked me to give him a lesson. Lulu was quite capable but you know how it is with husband or wife teaching each other.

It was early in the morning with dew still on the ground. We assembled and inflated the envelope with the petrol driven Fan then fired up the propane burner to heat it up. It is always a spine tingling feeling to see the balloon rise up and take shape. Just a small error with the direction of the burner flame which is approximately fifteen feet long and you can set fire to the whole side of the envelope, can be very expensive.

Edward and I took off out of the valley and soared over the Surrey Hills. This part of the country is covered mainly by pine trees because of the sandy soil. We eventually flew over the Hogs Back which is the six mile long chalk hill that runs between Guildford and Farnham. It was named the Hogs Back many years ago because it has the curvature of a hog's back. (Pig's) Having passed over this hill the soil becomes clay and gravel the result being there are plenty of oak trees growing there.

Edward decided to land in the corner of a field which was close to a road and there was a gate where the retrieve crew and Lulu were waiting. Having landed I stayed in the balloon while Edward and the crew walked the balloon to the gate. We found that the gate was locked. To save lifting the balloon and equipment over the gate when it is a dead weight and heavy, I proposed that I fly the balloon over the gate while the crew held the fifty foot long rope that had been paid out on the now very wet grass. This had been done many times before without any problems.

I had elevated the balloon to just above the gate when a strong gust of wind came down the hill wrenching the rope out of the crew's hands. Normally this would not present a problem it would be just a case of landing in the next field. I was now flying with fifty feet of wet rope hanging below the balloon. I was not unduly worried and prepared to fly over the woodland ahead of me.

Then I saw the high tension electric wires at the edge of the wood just a short distance away and running directly across my path. We had not seen them as they were at the same level as the trees. This effectively hid them from view. At the speed I was now travelling I realized that I could not climb quick enough to stop the trailing rope dragging over them. The rope was wet and would easily transmit the electric current up to the balloon basket. This would cause the propane tanks to explode. I did not fancy the idea of being cremated this way as I was feeling very much alive.

I looked to see if I could release the rope quickly but there was not a quick release, it was tied securely. I thought that I could pull the rope into the basket quicker than trying to untie it. Hand over hand I pulled it into the basket at the same time turning my head to look at the electric cables getting closer and closer. I was trying to estimate whether I could leave any rope hanging below the basket, then realized I could not chance it. At the same time I knew I was losing height as I had not left the burner on as I could have done. But that was an after-thought. I had thought the envelope was hot enough. There is always a danger if you let go of the burner controls when the balloon is swinging in a gust of wind as it is on gimbals and can set fire to the balloon envelope.

At this point I knew I could get the rope into the basket and just clear the wires but the result would be that I would hit the trees. This did not unduly worry me as I had often landed in tree tops to imagine what it was like to be a bird, and then sit there to view the scene.

I hit the top of the last oak tree on the far edge of the woods. In front of me was a large grass field. This was not a controlled landing and I crashed deep down into the oaks thick foliage. When I say crashed there was a loud crashing and cracking of branches. The basket seemed wedged firmly like a little tree house and the envelope was leaning out into the field with the light breeze. I intended to let the envelope collapse safely into the field and retrieve the basket later. But then the basket fell sideways and I was in danger of falling about forty feet.

I said a few choice swear-words and decided to put bursts of heat into the envelope from this acute angle, I might burn the envelope but the dangerous position I was in convinced me. Slowly with little quick bursts the envelope rose up and pulled me upright and then slowly started lifting out of the tree, stripping leaves and twigs as it tore itself out of the grasp of the branches.

As I flew away across the field I could see an excellent field to land in with open access to the Guildford to Aldershot road. After landing I studied the situation. I was up to my waist in leaves and a bloody great branch that was sticking up out of the leaves which was as thick as my arm. I had landed about one hundred metres from the road into the field.

A young man came cycling over to me, I knew that Edward and Lulu would be arriving very soon and would be anxious about the state of their expensive new balloon and perhaps wold have some concern about my welfare. The youth was intrigued by the leaves that I had collected. It looked rather like a "Hop tally basket full of a bushel of Hops." I said to this young man "Do me a favour and quickly gather these leaves and hide them in the ditch over there and I will give you a couple of quid".

The young man rushed back and forth using his jacket as a wrapper to carry the leaves as I closed down the propane tanks and burner. The balloon was still inflated but the basket was clear of leaves and branches when the retrieve crew arrived with Edward and Lulu. They did look very concerned and after inspecting the basket they still had looks of curiosity on their faces. They had probably seen the balloon hit the trees and yet I was at ease and at peace with the world.

The young cyclist was grinning as he was happy with three quid and our secret. Their balloon was in a pristine state; curioser and curioser (Quote from Alice in Wonderland) because I felt I was in wonderland. There was never any discussion about the flight or my near miss of the high tension wires or disappearing into the woods. It is this sort of fun that makes ballooning interesting.

SOMETHING WRONG ?

Wife and I on train
just I was offered a seat
She does look nurse-like

Senryu

OLD AGE Three Senru's

I can't eat onion's
I'll tell you about my illness
You know I am old.

I carry a phone
Talk a lot about Facebook
I Twitter, I'm young

They write, they line-dance
Tease and please, compose poetry
They are young at heart

THE DREAM

On the day I became too old to fly
Was the day life ended, I wanted to die
Walking the hills wondering what to do
when I came across a motley crew

They stopped and the leader spoke to me
"Are you lost? There is nothing here to see
Men, women all ages and children too
They all wore clothes of navy blue

My blue jacket I'd thrown on the ground
"May I have those, my clothes are as found?
You may have my jacket and my cap
for I no longer have any use for that.

They moved on leaving me alone, to think
this is the time that people turn to drink
Then I came across a decrepit shanty town
People had lived there, till law broke down.

It made me think of my clean, ordered life
My wife, structured work, very little strife
I then decided to come down from the clouds
and join the earthlings, the common crowds

This was a dream. Or was it?
One thing is certain I miss flying balloons
But fortunately found a new hobby, writing;

TO SAVE OR NOT TO SAVE

Many high priests of the past
had false ideas that didn't last
Men that controlled the economy
In their minds was, I, myself-me
Past priests were also politicians
they liked to behave like magicians

Today's monetary priests, like Merkel
are running in a never ending circle
A circle of inflation and deflation
which is no good for any nation
printing money has happened many times before
Countries printing paper money to go to war

Printing paper money is just a business franchise
Banks printing it to increase their power and size
Printing paper money is only a way to create
additional income to fund the Nation or The State
When governments create paper money injections
it causes financial problems, economic distortions

The public think money can be valued by indices
Governments use it to manage money by guesses
Paper currency is absolutely State controlled
Soon you'll find, you are not allowed to own gold
Central banks are buying things that are an asset
Then pay you with paper money while the ink is wet

Governments control money supply by intervention
It started in 12th Cent China. It's not a new invention
History shows it many faults and will create defaults
without the government holding gold in its vaults

When it all ends in tears and disastrous position
The politicians will of course blame the opposition
To spend or not to spend. That is the question.
One thing is sure in my mind I do not trust politicians

HAPPINESS

Material things do not guarantee happiness
Contentment does not depend on what you possess
Money can bring you food, wine and warmth
But not a lovers care in sickness and in health

Don't think that joy is in promiscuity, alcohol or drugs
That is the underworld of thugs and brainless mugs
Happiness is in seeing seeds that you did sow
To have children and see them learn and grow

Freedom to think without outside undue pressure
Having a mind that is kind, has value beyond measure
The ability to enjoy fresh water and the salty sea
and to be able just to walk, talk and feel free.

Authors Note I have dipped in the dark depths of depravity and have seen the problems that can and will emerge.

MEE-JING, TILLS RING

Flavour enhancer
or MSG flavouring
gives headaches

Haiku poem. Monosodium Glutamate, Mee-jing is what the Chinese call it.

GIVING GIFTS

When you see someone giving away
lots of money in goods or cash
Consider what's in it for them
and find out if the giver is rash

For most people particularly politicians
freely give away what is not theirs
Gift Aid and other funding abroad
will cost you, your kids and their heirs

If it's lottery money or personal assets
Or in a good cause, I do not care
Politicians are giving and spending
your earnings as if it was theirs to share

The Government is splashing cash
abroad in bundles far and wide
Money which costs just paper and ink to print
and will create a rich and poor divide.

Note. The British government has given millions to a private steel enterprise in India, which will be invested in mineral assets. This will increase in value while your printed money will diminish in value like the German Deutschmark did and the Greek Drachma.

Note.
In 1951 on the Greek island of Rhodes I paid 10,000 Drachma for a small cup of coffee, I expect you will be doing something similar soon.

PEOPLE POEMS & STORIES

NOTE. I LIKE WRITING ABOUT PEOPLE SO THE NEXT PAGES ARE ON THAT SUBJECT.

PERCEPTION BY PARTICLES

What I think is me and what is you
is purely a pile of chemicals and water
Held together by a mysterious glue

Life is how you imagine it should be
Your reality is not my idea of reality
You choose how it looks, what you see

Views of right or wrong change in time
Your ideas of love will be different to me
Other people's dreams will not mimic mine

Gluons neutrons subatomic particles
Protons hydrogen atoms, electrons
Truly, we are a strange pile of eclectic articles.

HAND WASH

Five pints of water
Mix with car dirt and rubbed
makes a grinding paste

Senryu.

BILL THE BAKER 1944. Bill Wilkinson

Bill was a big strong man that
lived in a village called Badshot Lea,
Cottage of hand-made bricks, oak cruck beams
This was where he owned a bakery.

His huge mixing bowl held a sack of flour,
Flour sacks weighed 220 lbs or more
I believe he was stronger than the Black-Smith,
He had to carry the sacks of flour to the upstairs floor.

To keep the dough warm to help it rise, there was a
wooden proving bin, to keep it in.
The loaves were placed in the oven with a long oar like
pole, sandwich bread was turned over in a tin

The wood fired oven, 2ft high 15ft long 10ft wide
built of beautifully built brick arches
In the evening, baking done, he filled the oven with faggots, Silver Birch swishy branches.

In the morning with a bit of paper he lit those sticks
now being very dry it burnt with ferocious heat.
Then with a mop he cleaned the floor of ash,
Scones cook first, then bread, cakes as it cooled, neat!

The bread tins went in upside down this put flecks of
ash in the crust, I found it rather nice
The proved loaf was turned over onto the paddle then
slid onto the bricks, a sprig of holly added spice

I collected twelve loaves and chewed around the crusts
while balanced on my bike handlebars and brakes,.
I wonder if customers thought mice had been nibbling
the bread. It was a better taste than cornflakes

One day while watching Bill mix the dough
Stripped to the waist, bent over the bin
sweat running from all over his body
and dripping from his arms and chin

I was only eleven years of age, but I said,
"Bill your sweat is going in the dough,"
He laughed, but didn't bother to wipe his brow
"Yes, it is salt; it makes for a better taste you know."

Note. The oven has been demolished but the house is still there. Faggots were bundles of birch tree branches. Many years ago yard brooms were made of those swishy branches.

TRAFFIC CONES

Have you wondered,
why so many traffic cones?
Each charged per hour!

Haiku poem.

EBOLA'S REACH

With Ebola effectively hiding for twenty-one days
It will be able to catch you in many ways
Closely packed people in a club, a cut or fighting
will be welcomed by this virus that likes bleeding
Shaking hands might end up as a curse
A nod might have to do, that can't get worse

The French have always kissed the cheek
This virus can enter shaving cuts, kill the weak
It might be wise not to have unprotected sex
And don't kiss your cat, it can pass from pets
People that chop and carry wood, cut their meat
A scratch can mean their maker they might meet

Is it on public transport. If it is you cannot tell
A cough or helping hand can mean a road to hell
The cockroaches survived the Dinosaur Extinction
Perhaps half our species might have that distinction.

Note. Those that wish to cross countries borders undetected could be ill, leaving the population unprotected.

TABOO'S

It is my firm view
Tattoo's will become taboo
Skirts go up and down!

Taboo-haiku.

STEVE THE CLIMBER
Stephen Edward Faherty

Steve is from Wales, has lots of tales
Enjoys the company of a pretty female
Runs up high hills and down the dales
Of Irish descent, lean and mean no fat at all
A tree climber, lumberjack, artist, woodcarver
Risks his life for hardly any reward at all

Excellent vocabulary, has nice turn of phrase
A hard worker, untidy, needs a woman
Lives in a caravan, very cold on winter days
Six feet tall, sharp features, reads a lot,
Money avoids him, so he does not gamble
Have not seen him drink alcohol or take pot

When at the top of tall trees
Like a sailor atop the high mast
He sways around in the breeze
He has fallen more than twice
Saved by his ropes and skill
Daily danger for low pay; Not nice.

Steven Faherty is also an artist and wonderful wood carver. He was kind enough to paint the cover for my book Building the Khufu Pyramid-Shedding New Light on the subject.

STEAM PRESSURE

I'm an old boiler
I've run out of good stories
has my fire gone out?

CARAVAN by the poet Anaisnais.
Anna-Marie Docherty.

Caravan, caravan,
taking me where er'e you can
A place to rest to relax, have fun
Whether in wind storm, rain or sun

To go anywhere we want to roam
to take a break away from home
Be it inland, town, woods or sea
hills or vales, you'll shelter me.

Anna wrote this poem for my wife and I as we operate a Caravan Club site between Guildford and Farnham.

IT MAKES YOU THINK

I read the following poem by Aesthete2000, USA.
It is called PERSPECTIVE. Very pretty flow of words but wait there is something missing; it makes you think. So I toss it round and round in my mind, like a salad dressing done with words not veg, it makes you think.

Now I find that underneath the cold print, cold like ice there, rages a river underneath. No better, I liken it to a plain looking Lava-plain, solid on the top but underneath a hot lava flow with all the ingredients to make, to create with all the myriad of molecules the likes of me, you and them. It made me think more than once, trice, even thrice.

PERSPECTIVE

Reflective
of considered opinion
relationship of facts and time
oriented to be objective
but humanly subjective

Effective
Transforming two dimensional planes
to imagined reality of depths and heights
vanishing and station point's respective
illusion by dots and lines connective

Directive
Making believable what is imaginable
teasing the mind to consider the improbable
fooling the eye of the most introspective
creating a view for the imaginative and selective

WONDER
Illusion
Conception of the mind
contradiction to the eyes
reality gone asunder

PONDER
Perception
The creation of the surreal
manipulation of lines
to infinity or just off yonder
distance to ponder
cause for wonder

SURMISE
Adventure
Sensation one conjures
realization capitalized
beyond each door a surprise
to enter upon or merely surmise

DRAMATISE
Mind travel
Preferred transportation
for spirits born to soar
actors on wings in disguise
everyday life to dramatize

FANTASIZE
Exploration
Beyond your comfort state
farther than ever imagined
possibilities to conceptualize
dreams to actualize

Art seen through my squinty eyes
for the heart to conceptualize
Art is all of the above; and more
as conceived by the thinking woman
proving compatibility of both sides of brain

Written by AESTHETE2000.

Note. She was my mentor from the USA that I met on Allpoetry.com

AUTUMN

The Autumn leaves adorn the trees
with colours to suit a King or Queen
Gold and yellow and shades in between
We aged humans tend to be more sedate
wearing drab colours, a rather dull display
of browns and blues, greens and grey

As the trees die in a blaze of colour in
a final show of absolute ostentation
A friend of mine dies in another nation
Aesthete2000; sadly a poet I never met
and yet I felt her warmth from so far away
This loss has left me feeling in total disarray.

Note. This lady helped me with my poetry and persuaded me to write, which has been a most interesting and rewarding experience for which I will be forever grateful to her. Sadly she has passed away but she is on my mind every day.

COLOURFUL LEAVES

Poetry words are like colourful leaves
drifting across spaces in your mind
Then like certain leaves that catch the eye
when written down in poem or prose
Disappear from short term memory
as quickly as those Autumn leaves
wisk away in the winter winds.

MARS

Mars, yes we all know it is there
And quite frankly I do not care
If it is very hot or horribly cold
or there is water or lots of gold

Here on earth, stars twinkling in the night
are obscured by a smog of scattered light
from street lamps always burning bright
I do not think that this is right

During this economic recession
why not learn such a simple lesson
and save electric consumption, plan it
Fit time switches, to help our planet

A rocket has just gone off to Mars
yet our children cannot see the stars
Mars is over nine months travel away
better to spend the money here, I say

Over one million youngsters out of work
mostly those that do not wish to shirk
The cost of just one exploratory rocket
would help many with an empty pocket

Does it all make sense to any of you
does it have any commercial value?
Why give all that finance and respect
There must be a hidden military aspect.

HOW OLD PEOPLE DISAPEAR

Have you noticed how the
Old people tend to disappear
The young do not listen to you
"You're talking history" they jeer
More so if you are going deaf
And cannot hear the 'Upper Clef'

Young children will only address you once
With no reply, they regard you as a dunce
What they do not realize, although not nice
Is that history repeats it's self twice or thrice
The old have seen it happen all before
Seeing the young in error makes them sore

Words and music always change with time
Youth tend to copy others, and toe the line
I as an Oldie I think that Rap is awful crap
When young I thought ill of Ballet and Tap
If you have a large yacht and Lamborghini's
Muscular men will abound and girls in bikinis

FELLING-FALLING-FAILURE

I studied the scene
then cut a vee in the tree
It fell the wrong way!

Haiku 5-7-5 Syllables

CAR DREAMS

Car adverts, will always show,
as if you will be on your own
Promising freedom to roam
Join the select club, be the one
Be part of the elitist throng
comfort, speed. How very wrong

Join the traffic jam, the long queue
No toilets for more than twenty miles
Need a pee, and sitting on aching piles
Fuming at the many miles of cones
One lane open, on the motorway
As two men are cutting the grass today

Your new sporty car is hard
to keep below that speedo red line
You pay the taxes, the tolls, and the fine
You'll need lots of cash at the Motorway Cafe
A must, do not fall asleep, "Have a break"
Expensive food and coffee, to stay awake

Adverts do not show, watching for cameras
Police bikes, radar traps, vans, unmarked car
You must though, or you will not get very far
I know you want to be Greener, Carbon Aware
But trains are not cheaper, and getting dearer
so you are forced by circumstance to keep her.

Note.
Governments lied about the benefits of diesel
to increase their tax revenue. Oil prices went
down drastically but petrol pump prices don't.

INTERNET DATING

There both hunting
they are looking on the web
each with their reasons

I look for a man
A handsome man with a job
One that I can love

I look for a girl
that I can make a victim
I pretend I'm rich

TRAFFIC CONES

Are you puzzled and annoyed by traffic cones
that line the roads for mile on mile
Like alien self-generating gnomes
And the police do not get involved or care
Why they are there everywhere stopping traffic,
leaving highways empty, bare

At the end of three of miles or so
There will be a solitary grass-cutter
On a wide verge wearing bright day-glow
Why are there so many of those cones?
Because each one is charged by the hour
Making money, so deaf to all your moans

Note. Health and Safety is used as an excuse

PHILLISTINE IN PHILLY. (Adult story)

My first visit was in a centenary year, when the Yanks were celebrating some historical connection or disconnection with the British and celebrated with a big tea party in Boston. The Brits were not invited and being unusually unkind stopped supplying decent tea. That is why the Americans started to drink coffee. Sorry, I digressed.

My son Bernie aged sixteen and I arrived in Philadelphia in July 1976 and stayed with a delightful couple with two young children. The very first day our hosts decided to give us every comfort and they decided to have a British Evening. The husband lit a big log fire while his wife cooked a typical English dinner.

The fire had been alight for some time, when the wife walked into the dining room to ask hubby to lay the table. She started screaming which hurt my ears and took everyone by surprise. Eventually her hubby realized she had put all the family silver, cutlery, coffee pot's etcetera under the fire grate. The ivory handles were burnt off and everything was black. With my training as a young commis waiter as to the cleaning of silver I salvaged the cutlery, but the coffee set was ruined.

Dinner was served. It was roast beef and potatoes, Yorkshire pudding and veg. We sat down in a hubbub of chatter. Bernie and I studied our carefully crafted meals in front of us, said grace and picked up our respective knives and forks in a slow deliberate appreciative fashion. Then, when placing a fork-full of meat and veg into our mouths we both realized that there was a deadly silence. Upon looking up we realized that none of the family had used the Knives and forks. But had loaded piles of meat and veg into very large bread rolls. There was no use for that lovely silver cutlery and they could not enjoy a laugh with us because their mouths were full.

Next morning after breakfast a car full of pretty female teenagers arrived looking for young Bernard. They had heard about the handsome young Brit and wanted to take him out. It was agreed and off he went in their car. We did not see him for three days and nights.

In the evening of the first day I was taken to a function being held in a Philly police club. I did not have a partner to dance with nor do I drink alcohol, so I amused myself watching people. Suddenly this big guy jumps up and comes towards me as he dives his right hand onto the gun under his right armpit. "What are you looking at" he demanded. "You" I reply, and he asks why.

I had been looking at his very attractive female friend but I did not think it wise to tell him that. So I said, "I was wondering how long you have been married?" "How long." he asked. When I told him three months, he grabbed me saying "Wow you are right." then he introduced me to his wife. He was a plain clothes cop. I asked him why there were gaming machines in the club? He said they had been confiscated. "Surely it was illegal in Philadelphia?" I asked. He told me it was for Charity. I looked at him, "For Police funds?" he nodded. Later he asked me if I would like to accompany him and his colleague on a patrol early in the morning. He told me to wear a suit. I agreed. In the morning I met him at the police station. He introduced me to his colleague and we set off in their car. Very soon they found a body on a parking lot by the side of the road.

My cop walked over to the body which was a woman lying face down. He hooked his boot toe under her and turned her over then called out, "Its Jane, a prostitute." Three more police cars arrived and they stood around, it did appear to be quite aimlessly. But suddenly the 'dead' body sat up and started yelling, "The bastard drugged and robbed me, Bastard". My cop started backing towards his car and signalled for me to do the same, but the Sergeant called out "Come back it's your job." "Oh, jeez Sarge No!" "Yes, get in your car". The sergeant then instructed the others to put Jane in the front passenger seat, she was still ranting about being robbed.

The sergeant studied his watch, "It is five to the hour, start up". "Oh Sarge!" "Start up, five, four, three, two, one, Go. The police car shot off at high speed with all the other officers laughing. "What's going on?" I asked his colleague. "Well, often prostitutes accuse us of abusing them, so if he drives at sixty miles an hour to her residence and back and it calculates at one mile per minute on his return. Then he would not have time to molest her would he." My cop returned in his car and they dispersed still amused by his agitation. Shortly after this there was a radio message about an armed robbery.

Why do the American police cars put their sirens on? It alerts the robbers. On arrival at the block of high class flats the two cops jumped out and started darting about from corner to corner. I sat there fascinated, because they looked and acted just like Starsky and Hutch. Perhaps you will not know that they were TV character, actor cops. Then the big guy ran over and said "Get out the car, you are a target sitting there looking like a Cop." They never found the armed robbers as I expect the robbers were not deaf.

That evening the Cop took me to a bar, I ordered a lemonade. The barman said "No." I asked why not and he replied, "We don't serve Queers." this was a derogatory term for 'Gay's in those days. I exploded into a verbal attack at this completely indifferent barman but he eventually gave in to accept me having a lemonade shandy. "Nope, we don't sell halves, you can have a pint." He said. So like a man's man I squared my shoulders and sipped at my big pint of shandy. I should have asked for a straw.

Then I heard clip-clop and nearly fell of my high stool when I looked down the bar. There was a beautiful naked woman walking down the top of the bar. Well not exactly naked, she had stilettoes on. Clip, clop-clip clop as she swung her slim hips side to side, her firm busts rising and falling in rhythm with her deliberate bouncy steps. Of course I averted my gaze as an English gentleman would be expected to, but she stopped right in front of me. She was not naked after all but had an itsy-bitsy piece of yellow ribbon tied with a string around her waist. I had never seen anything like this before and did not know what to do. My companion rescued the moment by putting a Greenback note under her 'G-string', as I now know it is called. She then danced most seductively for him, and of course I was allowed to look.

I had to rescue my young son Bernard from the clutches of those selfish girls and drive straight to the airport just in time to catch our plane. There was not even enough time to retrieve his luggage from the hosts. He came home in jeans and Bermuda shirt; he would only inform me that he had a marvellous time. So did I. He corresponded with one girl for quite a while but he never got back to see her again.

DAISIES

Daisies open their petals to welcome the sun
to use photosynthesis and be photogenic
Pleasing to see for bug, bee, you, me, everyone

Then they turn their heads to follow the light
until the sunset, when their life-light dims
then to close their petals for the night

The random patterns they create of white
against the background of green-green grass
with yellow spots is truly a delightful sight.

BREAKING AND ENTERING

I am so pleased to share this day with you
Sunny days are better shared, it's true
It's the first day of May, this year 2004
Won't be here again, never seen before
I tried to enter through a window light
and halfway in, found it extremely tight
Chest was stuck, my legs were off the floor
I cannot breathe, there are locks on the door

I think I am going to die, this first of May
Then I realize, don't panic It's the wrong day
My wife should be here to help, to watch
She's not and my trousers are up my crotch
Is that a damsel to rescue me? No, I wait.
Perhaps a friend, who will say "what's up mate"
Should I wait for someone to pull me out
If the law comes by I might get a clout

I recall a convict that was in the USA
He squeezed between bars and died this way
So with a heave, lifting up, I am free again
Falling back, luckily ground was soft with rain
Then armed with long pole of wood
moved the restraining prop, as now I could
and then after opening the large garage door
My Mercedes car went in, home once more

Note. I was lucky to escape from dying, it was late at night and nobody around.

My garage door got locked and could only be opened from the inside.

DYSLEXIC

She wrote that I was clever
nobody has ever called me
that in all my life. No not ever
It helps me with my self-esteem
although not sure why it was
said, perhaps it was just a dream

Being dyslexic, I skipped out of school
tired of teachers violence and sneers
Without diplomas, joined life's septic pool
After Merchant Navy, joined the Air Force
but after regarded as a hopeless case
Being discharged was my only recourse

Then three years as a Royal Engineer
helped to really change my life
learning without punishment or fear
I have changed my occupation
roughly every ten years, and
enjoyed life beyond expectation

In a life of meeting opinionated Clowns
that despised my lack of schooling
Many fights, lots of ups and downs
He said, " Only those that are intellectual
should live in this village, you should leave".
His pathetic plea to me was ineffectual

Three lovely children, two good wives
First twelve years, second one forever
Chauvinist pig, then a New man. Two lives
Two Café's, Skydiving Centre, Stone quarry
Two planes, Hot Air balloons, all past now
Lot of good times, some trouble , I'm not sorry

It was an American poet Aethete2000
that surprised me by calling me clever.
and encouraged me to write a book.

She did me the honour of writing an analysis
for the back cover of my first book

MY PLEASURE

A warm hand gently caressing
The suns warmth, a blessing
To feel the wind ruffling my hair
Rain in moderation, then fair

A warm safe place to sleep at night
To gaze at nature with gift of sight
A drink of cool fresh sparkling waters
To bear healthy sons and daughters

To be able to watch their growth
and hope they do not suffer sloth
Avoiding famine, pestilence and war
I wish such a lot, but nothing more.

A FAULT

If you look for faults
you will find it every time
So take rough with smooth

Senryu.

A GOOD HOUSE FIRE

In 2004 my younger son and his wife purchased a semi-detached house in a nice road in Aldershot by virtue it was in an excellent road, it was cheap and a good school was close by.

This house was built just after the Second World War and the garden had not been touched for about forty years, indicated by five thirty foot high Lawsonia trees which filled the small rear garden. They are the bushy evergreen trees that make excellent hedges but made this this little garden like a dense dark jungle. Hidden in this dark greenery was a collapsed wooden shed covered in a tarred fabric.

First my son asked me to put a cat-flap in the rear door. When I cut the hole I discovered that the door was made of a pressed type of cardboard and filled with straw. A door made in the war, not exactly burglar proof so we changed all the doors. Then I knocked down the shed and I took it all home to burn.

Next we altered the bathroom toilet arrangement to a single bathroom and found that the interior wall was eight inches out of square. Also the ceiling joists were all odd sizes, some being under two inches wide and others up to six inches wide. I can visualize the original carpenters being told. "There is a shortage of good timber me old mate; cos of the war!" Incidentally my elder son's house which was built in 1997 is accurate to millimetres.

Next came the trees. As I felled the first inner one, the old lady next door came shooting out like a spider towards the fly. "You mind my fence." She shouted as she examined her chicken wire type fence. Her garden was immaculate to the point that when my car tyre flicked a single stone into her front garden, she picked it up and threw it back.

One of the trees had grown into her fence so I left it to the last, Then starting at 8am one morning when my son was at work I cut above her fence and then became horrified when it fell the wrong way right across her garden. I looked up at her bedroom window, the curtains were still drawn.

I got a stepladder and climbed over with the chain saw and quickly cut the tree into small pieces and threw them back over the fence. Every-where there were piles of sawdust. I got a dustpan and a stiff brush then carefully swept it all up and climbed back over at 10am at 10.05 the curtains drew back and she came rushing out to inspect and luckily found nothing to complain about. I then took all of the felled trees and shed home to burn.

I waited until the farmer next door had cut and baled his hay then one evening I set fire to it. Wow! the lawsonia burns like oil and the tarred shed gave it some colour and fury as well. This fire was at the bottom of my woods where I had a paddock. There was a water tap there so I was not bothered too much.

The A31 Hogs Back road runs East to West on a hill about one and a half miles away to the North; I could see the lights of the traffic from Guildford. The flames were as high as the ancient oak trees and I was enjoying the spectacle and the myriad of colours from the tars on the shed when I was suddenly frightened that I was about to be abducted by aliens.

There were numerous strange blue and piercing bright lights moving through the woods towards me from different directions. Then I saw large figures in space suits and helmets with glaring eyes behind full face visors.

They surrounded me; then one spoke "What on this earth are you doing, you will set fire to the woods!" It was a fireman from Guildford. I had never observed them before clad in their protective fire proof clothing. I replied that I had water close by and the paddock was an effective firebreak.

Then another slightly differently clothed alien said "Oh, I thought we had a good house fire to deal with? As we came from Guildford over the Hogs Back we could see the flames and it really looked like a good house fire."
Then another piped up and said they came from The Farnham Station, and we could not find our way through the woods so we came on foot." Then all of them in a totally dispirited state trudged off back to their vehicles, so very disappointed that they never had a 'Good house fire.'

THE MAIL

Waiting debating
Is there anything in the mail?
Only spam Mam

Senryu.

A CARING CARER. My son's carer.

Of African ancestry as all can see
Her attitude is the best one could be

Never says an unkind word, sneer or snipe
She is naturally warm, touchy feely, cuddly type

Her laughter reverberates around the house, it's loud
She will always be noticed, stand out in the crowd

Being tall and with straightened hair
big brown eyes that delve deeply with her stare

Has a parental personality, palpably strong, she is rare
I'm so pleased that son is in her caring capable care

I was reduced to fits of laughter and happy tears
when I saw waxed paper tubes in Bernie's ears

Then it was set on fire to smoke and glow
at a cost of seven pounds fifty per go

Perhaps it's soothing and cleans his ears of wax
Cigarettes are bad for health, costs too much with tax

Emma does has a problem which makes me choke
She burns leaves rolled in paper, to watch it smoke

Note. Emma was my son Bernard's carer as he has Multiple Sclerosis. Those tubes were supposed to clear the wax in his ears.

DREAMS

This poem was written for my son who has Multiple Sclerosis; his name is A. B. Green (Bernie). I wrote as if I was in my son's position. Can you imagine what it is like to be very fit and active and then become paralysed?

When I am very tired, I sleep
and if fortunate, old friends I meet
Pals from school where I played Rugby
and ran in long races, cross country

Dreams of events, times long past
of riding motorbikes too fast
Dreams of childhood, damming streams
and home-made explosives, joyous screams

Of adventures just within the law
pushing my parents to the very last straw
Parachuting with the Parachute Regiment
Building dads house, covered in cement

Flying with dad in a Balloon over London
a mix of pure madness fear and fun
I became a motorbike cop, so glad
Wife, and three kids, now a granddad

Then I slowly awake, become conscious
I am now paralyzed by Multiple Sclerosis
My wife is my joy, my life, my life's crutch
and my children are such a joy to watch

Note. Bernie enjoyed a very full life riding fast motorbikes. Driving high speed police cars, Parachute jumped with the Parachute Regiment and flew hot air balloons and still had time for a multitude of other things such as Chairman of the local MS Society.

WHY AM I HERE

Why am I here? This question puzzled me
Luckily, there is so much to do and see
It made me forget about the question
which is a pre-occupation of religion

I have enjoyed most of my long life
Despite times of hardship and strife
While I am here, I try to bring cheer
To those around me and that are near

It appears that we need some stress
to keep us straight, out of a mess
The trouble with 'Man' he thinks he's superior
Species, when too many become a pest, inferior

Nothing will ever explain why we are here
So as you'll never know, relax; have no fear.

Note.. The further you look into space the more you should realize how insignificant we are. And how lucky you are to be able to think, see, feel, communicate and share your experiences with your fellow living creatures.

LOVE CAN CHANGE (Adult)

Sex, making babies is called mating
It is not love, it's recreating
Love is separate from sexual pleasures
I will try and explain with different measures
Love can grow, slow, change, dim and diminish
Love can lead to marriage, change and finish
I loved my mother all my life from a child
Except while as a teenager, when I was wild

I loved the adrenalin of the sexual chase
with the urge to increase the human race
I loved the fear of sky-diving, pulsating high
But I certainly did not have a wish to die
Loved my sons with a ruff tuff love, that's rough
Love for my daughter is soft, though she is tough
Love can diminish, disappear, married twice
We learn from errors, mistakes, it will not be thrice

Love must be nurtured, not allowed to freeze
Or it will drift away, fly away on a breeze
Love is not permanent undying, or has clarity
It must be reflected, worked at with parity
Love can have different levels, shades aspects
I love my cat, he responds, talks, it reflects
Love, keeping it and the enemy away, a war
Keep some ammunition, stay awake, don't be a bore

Love of my wife is reflected in how she shares
The worries we meet in life, it shows she cares
I know that this cannot cover matters all
But I must close now, I heard my wife call.

"Coming Darling."

SEEKING PERFECTION

Life is never perfect
as there always will be strife
Mine is perfect right now, all due to my wife
In all walks of life and business
there will always be Ups and Downs
People can't be perfect, you will always meet clowns

We have lost lots of money, due to dodgy people
but I am content and do not have regrets
As at the moment we do not have any debts
I believe there is a Creator of the Universe
and feel Christian but never go to Church
I'm a Zen Buddhist; don't leave people in the lurch

I was so lucky to have been born in England
in between the World Wars, so sad
to see Wars started with so little cause
We are so fortunate to live in this blessed country
Small Great Britain; protected by the Gulf Stream
Such a pleasant place, so fertile, so very green.

2015.

BEING OLD

A fresh coat of paint
why? The house is warm and dry
and soon I shall die!

Haiku.

PERHAPS.

Perhaps, it was all meant to be, for me
A tough time, too much salt
showed me how to live, you see.

As a child, being the eldest boy
I was used for parenting practice
First being the parents training toy

Perhaps, not knowing what to do with me
they became terribly frustrated
smacking does not help you see

Unfortunately for them and me
I wet the bed. I tied my winkle
with string, It didn't stop the pee

Perhaps, my father was a masochist
He enjoyed teaching discipline
it was not drink; never saw him pissed

World War 2 made things very hard
German planes overflew, bombs boomed
I got whipped if I didn't clean the yard

Perhaps as they didn't know dyslexia was at play
Teachers often whipped and punched me
I disappeared, staying away all day

Come back now and you'll get one, or six
if you run away. My dad meant whacks
I had to select the appropriate swishy sticks

Perhaps I was a chauvinist, Marriage did not last
Three lovely kids though, boy, girl, boy
Re-invented myself and deleted all my past

Because there was, and is no animosity
My ex-wife, children and new wife can mix,
and got along together quite happily.

SADLY, KNOW I KNOW.

I chased after a lady for one hundred feet
to offer my parking ticket for the street
Now I know that I am very old
for after that short run, I was told
Thank you Sir, with a smile she said
but now you had better go to bed
I am sure that she said this in jest
After that run, you had better rest

16/06/13. I will not forget this Father's day.

CHINESE FACE

I enjoy your face
When your smile brightens your eyes
my heart beats faster

Senryu. My wife.

LANGUAGE

Chinese Café worker
Irishman ordered breakfast
Take your "Fork-n-knife"

Senryu poem about my wife.

DOUGAL 1998

I have a friend, a mate, called Dougal
is always short of dosh, no, he is frugal
Dougal is not his given name
but suits him, with his shaggy mane
Lives at the home of his elderly mother
no wife or girlfriend, no bit of the other
He is always at the Car Boot and Auction
if you are going to bid, act with caution

Broken things, he always bids to buy
items that would make your mother cry
People look and talk, "Does he have a clue?"
they have not seen his saw and pot of glue
Chairs, tables with missing trim
you and I would put them in the bin
One leg missing from the chair
it will be ready for the Thursday Fair

The Auctioneer will describe to one and all
"Victorian," it echoes round the hall
His description in a theatrical whisper
to Frank, stage right, "This is a cracker
I am sure it is Arts and Crafts or Deco."
"Shut up, down there." his voice will echo
The chair he bought for £2 at Tuesdays Mart
now makes £20; I think that he is very smart.

Note. This used to be called 'Toms' Auction which was held in the evening at the Sea Cadets hall in Badshot Lea, Aldershot.

MY BAZOOKA

When I was 15 years of age, just before I left school, Wait a minute let me tell you something about that last school. I went to East Street School in Farnham Surrey and expected to leave at the age of fourteen but then I was told I had to do another year and was being sent to a school that had just been built. It was called Heath End Secondary Modern School which is on the outskirts of Aldershot.

When all the new students arrived at this school the builders were still there. I noticed straight away the difference in procedures. At East Street we would stay in the same classroom and the teachers would know you all personally, too personally my view. At Heath End we walked into the first class and a roll call was taken. After the first lesson and all subsequent lessons the students moved from class to class and the teachers stayed put. After an incident with a maths teacher who said I was cheating because I solved a maths question without the traditional system of working and writing out the equation. I decided to register at the very first class and then bugger off for the rest of the day, every day.

Occasionally I got pressganged into fixing the coat hangers into the cloakrooms and also spent some time digging a fishpond for the school which seemed the headmasters dream project. It is only last week I met an ex pupil that was working on that pond with me and made me think about it. I only ever played one game of football at this school and gave up after heading the ball. It was a heavy leather ball and the leather lacing cut my forehead, but for some reason I was voted Captain of Cobbett House. I did not do much to earn the title.

While I was playing truant and rambling around the countryside I acquired some powerful banger fireworks. They were called Crow-scarers and the local farmer called Mr Jim Tice hung them on burning ropes. As the ropes slowly burnt, it ignited the firework which exploded with a loud bang and scared the crows and pigeons. I found they were very powerful, for example I found they could blow a heavy metal dustbin lid higher than our house.

I had spent a lot of time with the soldiers that had been billeted in our village and I owned a 4.10 shotgun and a .22 rifle until I lost them when our guest house called Homefields in Runfold. It burnt down on the 4th February 1950, there is a Sand quarry there now. Apparently my father was made bankrupt on the 9th of February 1951. I learnt this fact in February of 2016.

It was in 1949 that I decided to build a Bazooka which was a term used by the military for an early rocket launcher which they fired from resting on the shoulder. I obtained a one inch diameter galvanized water pipe that was about five feet long from my grandfather, he was a plumber and blacksmith. I had watched him put a thread on pipes so I did that and closed off one end. Then I acquired some roofing nails. Now these nails had one inch wide heads and they fitted perfectly into the barrel, also they were about three inches long and heavy. I fired my bazooka a few times but I could not see where the nails were going to.

My uncle came across to me in the Café car park and asked what I was doing. He was only two years older than me, he then volunteered to get behind a roofing sheet of galvanized iron while I shot at it, and he would tell me if it hit the iron. Now bear in mind this was not thin tin, this was thick and heavy stuff. He got behind it and I walked about fifty yards away. I loaded aimed and fired, I never heard a clang of metal hitting metal.

I walked over to where my uncle was still squatting looking at a hole in the metal. The nail had gone sideways clean through the metal! It was a good job that he had sat down as it had passed very closely over his head. It would have killed him had it hit him.

I continued firing my bazooka until one day it fired prematurely and skinned my finger as I was loading the nail. I fared better than the boy that lived in the Jolly Farmer Pub as he blew some fingers off with an explosive made from some farm fertilizer. I was very happy to hear about that as a short time previously he had thrown half a house brick at me because I was sitting on his parents pub wall and it knocked one of my font teeth out It was justice I thought.

I met Mr Jim Tice in September (2012) when he purchased by book Dunce or Dyslexic and then by chance met his sister Monica Jones. I told them both about their fireworks and my bazooka.

Note. My elder son Bernie outdid me by building a large cannon at his private school and firing it at the school. Fortunately, the shot went over the building. This story is *Gunpowder, Plots and Plod* in *Dunce or Dyslexic* by Simpleton.

MANKIND.

Man has a problem
The trouble with humanity
is there are too many

Senryu poem.

GIVE AND YOU WILL RECEIVE

If someone gives, with a motive in mind
they will grow bitter and twisted, un-kind
Giving gives me genuine warmth within
does not have to be restricted to kith and kin

A child's twinkling eyes, a smile of joy
is sufficient when you give a toy
Birds freely give voice with song and call
the human listener feeds them in the fall

It is true, give and thou will receive
unless it was in preparation to deceive
I have not read the Bible right through
but what I now believe, may be true

It's the meek, not the brigands band
that will inherit this, our lovely land
I always wanted to see African folk and fauna
but could not bear to witness people's trauma

I remember Bible reading as a child
thinking of meek, being weak, mild
But now I realize it means in interpretation
not about strength, but mild, with education

AN ACT OF NATURE

Horse poo everywhere
done without a backward glance
Dogs doo, you can't do.

Haiku. Acts of nature with an Act against one.

IDEAS OF HEAVEN

Eight people arrived at the pearly gate
they were from varied countries or state
They were asked to choose partner or a mate
then to choose one shining coloured gate

It ended none of them were happy with their fate
They chose a partner of the opposite sex, a mate
and of the same nationality and colour
as learning another language was too much bother

The Africans chose the red gate as it was hot and bold
The Nordic people chose Blue as it looked icy cold
Europeans chose the Green as it was temperate
The Arabs never got a choice, they got the purple gate

Africans wanted to leave as there was poverty and war
Arabs wanted to move as there was no water to pour
Nordic's wanted sun and to wear big sunshine hats
Europeans wanted to get away from the Eurocrats

(There was not a Yellow gate as it was already full of Chinese.)

THE DANCING QUEEN.

The dancing queen has a beautiful face
a fine example of the English race
With large brown, laughing eyes
pink rose petal skin that cause men's sighs

Sparkling white teeth in straight line
set behind bow shaped lips so divine
Natural brown hair, slick healthy, shining
arched eye-brows, forehead with no worry lining

On her nose was a silver ring
I suppose it's considered, the in-thing
I told her she was a lovely English rose
but the ring drew attention to her nose

Then felt impelled and had to mention
that it distracted men's rapt attention
from studying her excellent good looks
And then I got into her mother's bad books

Saying, you think it's an improvement, it's not
at a quick glance, it looks like dripping snot
A true event, I can get away with it as a rule
as I'm speaking from the heart, an old fool.

Note. I met this young lady called Jackie at Line Dance classes. She is a professional dancer. She laughed at my statement but I thought her mother was going to explode.

HEY YOU, GOOD LOOKING
An example of modern English..

Tell me summink, tell me the truth
Do you think that I am a bit uncouth?

Don't ya like me latest dancing dress
Or is it cos me air's in a bit of a mess

I've really got a lovely big firm bot
Unfortunately it don't get touched a lot

I reckon my big breasts are the best
Ow about givin them a firmness test

Perhaps you think that ise still too thin
But you aint yet felt the warmth within

Perhaps you don't like the fag in me gob
But I don't do drugs, I'm not a nob

I wanna be me, just the real me
And have you always next to me

When you taste ma cooking, you'll feel a king
Then at scrawny women you'll stop looking

Ere let me get me mitts on you, don't struggle
Let me show you how I can lurve and cuddle

When you've touched me pale porcelain skin
And felt the deep desire that I have within

I will make you salivate with a dream
of my peach pie with cherry and cream.

BATU CAVE
A TOURIST ATTRACTION.

Malaysia, this country is a most interesting place
Batu Cave is huge and high up in a cliff face
Coaches packed with tourists eagerly arrive there
anxious to see the festival (Thaipusam) and enjoy the Indian fare.

Colourful Indian foods set out on stalls and tables
Spicy to entice thee, Pamphlets on the local fables
Ladies in Saris with long black tresses, selling cotton dresses
Men with hairless legs selling to people of foreign addresses

Steps up to the cave rise high up in the humid air
Those with disability and pensioners give up in despair
Flocks of pigeons patrol in packs, coo and plaster poo
Intent on annoying and anointing those there to view

I climb, slipping sliding on slippery steps to view
holding the hand rail peppered by pigeons too
I look over the hand-rail to find a safe track
There was a sinuous shiny snake, all black

A raging river at the bottom of the cliff base
Full of detritus, detrimental to the human race

I did make it to the top, full of anxiety (272 steps) The cave is huge, a great sight to see. This river is a floating plastic trap it should be all collected there before floating out to sea.

Written in 2011.

ATTITUDE

It happened many years past
But a valid tale will last
It's about attitude and manner
Language, life, position and grammar
I was untidy, unkempt, in dirty working clothes
I'd been cleaning toilets, drains bins, all of those
I owned Alf's Café. This was a transport café
This is the story of a policeman's verbal gaffe

My occupation would be described as caterer
Rising at 4am to bake, I am the café baker
Mid-day, cleaning floors toilets bins, all of those
Drains are blocked; I require rods and a hose
I hurry down the old A31 in my old car
Police stopped me before I had gone far
"What's the hurry 'Mush' where you running to?
"You're booked," and note book flicked through

"What for," I asked. He gasped "Speeding Mush,"
As he pushed me off the road into a bush
I replied, "I know why you picked on me
It was the gypsies that you were sent to see
They were at the transport café in Runfold
I'm an easier target, as I am alone and old,"
"Name and address and don't give me any tosh."
I quoted my name and address, which is very posh

His reaction was surprising, "Thank you Sir,"
I will look at the café to which you refer

Note. He closed his notepad, turned away and left to attend the incident to which he was sent.
The term 'Mush' was a derogatory term.

217

MR DULL

He was quite tidy, big build and tall
Like a six foot plain brick wall

No character in his face, it's like a ball
Shows no emotion, no features that I recall

Like the moon, he hardly lights up the room
Just a pleasant presence that lifts the gloom

Conversation is limited to TV films or footy
Did speak of wanting a motorbike, a Malagutti

Did not ask questions, no information to share
Like the wall it is solid, it's there but it is bare

Any interests? I did not tend to ask
Posing a question, seemed too much to ask

He smoked a large briar pipe with curved stem
Nodded to speakers, as if he understood them

Puffing the pipe allowed him not to speak
which might have shown his intellect was weak

Note. A stranger in a coffee bar.

THE DIFFERENCE

I enjoy the sight of Sheiks and Bedouin
Toureg wearing flowing coloured robes
I'm intrigued by the hair and hats of
Orthodox Jews with black clothes
The Rastafarian colours and decorates
his dreadlocks, demonstrating masculinity
Moslem faiths females favour veils and
Hijab's demonstrating faith and femininity

Sikhs are satisfied, showing their solidarity
by wearing smart silken turbans
All these faiths display their following
as do sporting teams and their fans
Christians tend to blend, difficult to define
Sometimes they proudly wear a small cross
The religious wear their clothes with pride
But a cross in the UK, can cause a job loss

HER ABSENCE

The silence is not
altered by the television

The coldness is not warmed
by hot drinks or heat.

26th November 2013

Note. My wife was in hospital.

ARTIFICIAL INTELLIGENCE

I thought he was intelligent
But that thought soon went
The I-pod never left his clammy clutch
I realized that it was his mental crutch
Unfortunately it makes him, out of touch
with people, by not communicating very much
While in a group his head was always down
Eyes never met, he had a permanent frown
Oblivious to his surroundings, often on Skype
Lost in the Internet, in a dream-world of hype
Life is not in Facebook, Skype or Twitter
Acumen is not playing with a computer
Making your I-pod a mental crutch or tool
Can end up making you look like a fool.

GREECE

Thinking of the Debt
Greece might be a Russian Port
Grease my palm or else

Haiku. Watching you. 2015.

MARRRIED LOVE

Love and compassion
necessities, not luxuries
with-out them, love dies.

Senryu.

BLACKIE

Blackie, is a true through and through Gypsy
He is very strong but not very tall
His perspicacity and powerful personality
Is much bigger than us all

Born in a horse drawn caravan and
as a child he slept and lived underneath
Parents travelled for work farm to farm
In the winter they lived upon the heath

Trousers held by leather belt and red braces
On his head always wears a brown trilby hat
Big brown highly polished leather boots
Looks tough, a softy really, wouldn't kick a cat

Didn't learn to read and write but take care
He might give you a sharp sideways kick
Not with those expensive polished boots
A quick wit and tongue does the trick

Picked potatoes, hops and all types of fruits
Stacked corn sheaves, children never came to harm
Cooked hedgehogs in clay, to hold the spines
Baked potato in ashes. A Life with charm

A NEW VENICE

People are building on the sand
Global warming, the sea will rise
creating a new Venice in Florida.

Senryu.

EYE OF THE BEHOLDER

She wears dingle dangle earrings
an ugly tattoo on each slender arm
A silver ring spoils her pretty nose
and wears plastic nails with stars
Assorted rings adorn the fingers
there are gold ones on her big toes
Wiggling, showing shapely legs and ankles
making her jewellery jiggle and jangle
When speaks, her tongue button glows

I think the human body unadorned
in its natural state and form is beautiful,
unless broken by bombs or blows
People are led and controlled by fashion
They wish to be different, but they are not
just following where the common herd goes
A tattoo can serve a useful purpose
A diabetic or organ could have one
On their fore-arm, where it shows

Or a warning message to doctors
saying, Do not resuscitate me.
so that your wishes, everyone knows
Surgery makes women look like dolls
hair, lipstick, lashes are enough to adorn
Character appears in facial lines, it shows
beauty is not in skin scarring, or metal rings
It is in personality mentality and deeds
it is not instant, it develops and slowly grows.

Note. A straight tree-trunk is boring. An old oak tree is very interesting as it is knurled and twisted. Plastic surgery removes the character from an older face.

LOVE, SEX AND MARRIAGE (Adult)

Love turns by anagram into vole
It can often disappear down a hole
Love is not sex, sex is not love
True emotion flies high, a cut above.

Pop songs of love like desert fall flat
Devoid of high feeling, who wants that?
Most modern songs cannot show
The true taste of how love can grow

In a marriage, a joint venture to tread
Always trouble shared, lifts the heavy head
This is where you will find loves highest peak
But it is not the path that all men seek

Some dream of loves lost in the past
Or dream of tying virgins to their mast
True love, like waves surges up and down
You must ride the turbulent sea of love or drown.

Marriage will never be a smooth path or road
Often you will have to carry a heavy load
But with all trouble and burdens shared
You will never be overcome or scared.

BEING GENEROUS

Generosity
is very often misconstrued
Better to be mean.

Senryu

MAN, IF SHE COULD BE THE ONE
By A-M. Docherty.

Tell her you love her,
reassure her
Hold her close and cuddle her
Treasure her

Go see her,
no matter how far away she lives
Always make an effort
let her know she is worthy

Let her know
that she is beautiful to you,
worthy of your love
Hold hands and kiss her

Be unpredictable
Send flowers, love cards
tokens of love, letters
and appreciation

Repeatedly
visit her when sick
Be there for her always
Hold her when sad or upset

Do not be afraid
to show your feelings
Nor share your hearts desires
Share secrets with her

Spend time together,
relax, have fun and laugh
Give up your seat,
tidy up and play your part

Open doors for her
Guard every word and breath
Make sure she gets home safe with a call;
better still see her home to the door

If you'd give your life for her
die for her, defend her, protect her
Then wait for her,
however long it takes

The sex can wait
Man, if she could be the one
with whom to share a life-time together
Respect her

Author Note
I only just noticed that if you take first word of each line
in the last stanza/verse, you get-
The Man with Respect.

© anaisanais A-M Docherty.

Note.
Anna-Marie was very kind to me
when I started writing poetry
She lives in Wales so we never met
I found her poetry on the internet.

MALFUNCTIONING

Once more without sleep
all dreams exhausted
Neurotransmitters on high alert
rekindling furious flames
that lap hungrily through mid-back to feet
Like a chippy chiselling wood on the lathe
I splinter and crack - screaming for regression
Just as a computer malfunctioning
I await time for reboot of my system
brief medical intervention -
some respite peace and solace
that in the whole of life
taken as one performance of the arts
it is but a musical interlude
short-lived in high anticipation of entr'acte

Author Notes on terms used:
solace - relief from emotional distress/source of comfort
interlude - short period of transition-
break entr'acte - between the acts

Poem by © anaisanais A-M Docherty.

STRESS.

People get stressed
when illness causes trauma
Try to understand

Senryu. by B.Green

CATARACT

A hood over the head
oxygen pumped under
My right eye is exposed

To occupy my mind
I pretend I'm in a tent with
light streaming through the hole

Liquid is squirted
The eye is numb
but the brain races

A nice nurse holds my hand
Her hand is small and warm
like my mother's tender touch

Snip-snip-snip-snip
like a leafcutter ant
The lens is removed

Glaring light fills the space
slowly a lens is slid in
The warm hand has gone

I ask, Is it stitched or glued?
his reply surprises me
Pushed in like a bottle cork

Next day I remove the pad
to find I have wondrous vision
and colours not seen before.

B.G. 2016.

A RHYME ABOUT LYME DISEASE.

On a lovely hot summers day
when on the grass you love to lay
Bugs, and deer tick, a beastly thing
lay waiting for a warm body to cling

Some just want to bite and disappear
leaving large red bumps on your rear
But the Deer Tick unnoticed, walks around
until a succulent vein to suck from is found

After applying an anaesthetic; digs down in your skin
leaving its rear end sticking out; with its head within
If you do not notice it or have a sense of unease
After two days you might have contracted
      Lyme disease

Dartboard red rings emanate from the wound site
This shows you might have the disease, from the bite
Don't delay if a deer tick digs deep in you
For Lyme disease can paralyze you. It's true.

Note. It was in March that the bug bit me, I was on powerful antibiotics for two weeks.

I wrote this as not many people realize how bad a bite from this tick can be and it is becoming more prevalent in the UK. I met a friend of Mike Turner a Parachute Regt man that got bitten when on honeymoon in the USA and now cannot walk.

Note. Wherever deer are the ticks will be on the grass and on the bushes they will attach themselves to any warm blooded creature.

COCKNEY SLANG.

Cockney rhyming slang is on
its last bacon and eggs
If you are not a Londoner
you'll be confused, its last legs
Londoners have been using it
for donkey's ears
which my interpreter says
means for many years

Do not assume that I am
a deep fat fryer
I have it on authority
that means a liar
And do not assume I'm
having a bubble bath
My dickie bird, that is word
is that it means having a laugh

Regarding bread and honey (money)
we lost our white Lady Godiva
which was the large white
five pound, paper fiver
Having expounded these thoughts
I'll don my weasel and stoat (Coat)
to buy a beer, a pigs ear
this rabbit has given me a sore throat

I will watch the custard and jelly
sitting in my Barrack Obamas
My teapot lids(kids) are amused
by my Stars and striped pyjamas.

I wrote this for and sent to Aesthete2000.

POETIC ATTITUDE

I have atti-chewed
you have atti-tood
Neither can you say nyther
and continue with neether

We duel over shed-uel
you will fight for sked-uel
In lieu of saying Leftenant
you fight for the lootenant

Our garage is english Gaa-raj
yours a french version Garidj
We properly pronounce Toma-toe
You improperly say Tomay-toe

Chips, you have to Frenchy-fy
to an absurd French Fries, why?
The letter Z is not Zee
It is definitely Zed, you see

So Zebra is Zeb-bra
not silly Zee-bra
and Bouy is pronounced Boy
not Boo-ee, more like ahoy

Nuclear cannot be Nukil-ar
it's New-clear, is that clear
Iraq, irritably spoken as Eye-rak
is irrefutably in English, I-rack

I am not adverse to say Vayze
for there is not an R in Vase
No need for risible ree-search
I agree to differ, after my research.

This poem was written and sent
to Aesthete 2000 in the USA for fun.

DEAR-OH-DEAR

Dear can sound formal, or sometimes polite
May even be sardonic which just isn't right
A homophone turns it into venison or Bambi
Sometimes just sounds a bit namby-pamby
So let's stick with 'Hi', an excellent choice
One that can be projected with confident voice.

Note.
Does anyone say 'namby-pamby' anymore? It seems to have disappeared from popular use. The term was actually coined 280 years ago to ridicule the poetry of Ambrose Philips by his contemporaries Alexander Pope and Henry Carey.

SWEET FA. A sad story.

Fanny is not a name that you hear any longer for a young lady as it seems to have developed into a derogatory term for part of the female body.

But in Victorian times it was a known name. You might if you are very old remember a film called Fanny by Gaslight which was a truly frightening film, where Fanny was frightened by the dimming of the gas-light.

Have you heard someone saying' 'I have Sweet fanny Adams' meaning, I have 'Sod all' or 'Fuck all.' Later it was abbreviated to 'Sweet FA." This did not mean sweet football associates. It meant having nothing to show for your efforts nothing, or nothing left!

This saying originated in August 1867 in the small farming town of Alton in Hampshire when a young girl called Fanny Adams aged eight years went for a walk by the river that runs through the centre of the town.
The river rises from a spring in the fields to the North of the town flows under the High street and still supplies the brewery. In those days it was a pleasant walk by the sparkling river running between the Hop fields and shaded by trees.

Unfortunately she was met by a young man called William Cheney aged 29 that worked as a solicitor's clerk. He persuaded her to accompany him and then killed and butchered her so completely that people said that there was nothing left of her. It took days for search parties to find all her body parts.

The British Royal Navy issued a new type of rations in 1869 which consisted of chopped up mutton in large rectangular tins. I suppose it looked like Corned beef in big rectangular tins. They made themselves mess tins from those cans. The sailors obviously did not think much of these rations calling it "Sweet Fanny Adams"

Even the modern manufactured naval mess tins are still called "Fannys" but I imagine that not many Royal Navy sailors realize how this name came into use.

GROWING OLD

The trouble with growing old
are all the aches and pains
and no insurance when you travel
Quite often I have found that
pension plans that you have made
and long term investments just unravel
We imagine that we are in charge
of our destiny, position in life
and always try to break the mould
We are just like sheep being driven
by forces we cannot comprehend
and unwittingly do as we are told
There is quite an element of luck
for I have lost many friends
on the journey to this fold
Calculated risk is better
than wrapping up in cotton wool
Then to children your stories unfold
People like to think of living forever
but there is no room for this
There is not enough room on earth
It is an obvious unwelcome truth
that you and I must die
to enable renewal in others birth
If there is no development or change
everything stagnates, rusts and rots
even the stars eventually explode
Everything in the universe re-cycles
In a trillion years or so you might
reappear as a humble nematode
If you are still alive at fifty-five
don't be a couch potato
Before your spirit flies away
Enjoy the scene, family and friends

Work at enjoying each moment
of every minute of every day
For some that died so young
I do not shed my tears
they enjoyed the sporting risks they took
Others have died; that took no risks
There is no balance sheet between good or bad
or everlasting credit for being good, in my book.

THE MONEY MAN

Poor Peggy said she had a proposal
But it was from a man of ninety three
She asked, why do only old men fancy me
When you left me in the hotel lounge
This ancient bore acting like a Toreador
offered to take me onto the ballroom floor

He told me of the world cruises he takes
and his house in the Cote d'Azur in France
Money made him think he had a chance
He said his wife of twenty-six years
Was in a Nursing Home after a stroke
and he was lonely, what a nice bloke!

He tried his luck with you dear wife
Cos he couldn't imagine we are married
Because I do not look bored and harried
I open doors for you, hold your coat
Share drinks with you and morsels of food
These are the things that are misconstrued

KEEPING YOUR MAN OR WOMAN

A gold ring and a wedding do not make a marriage
Nor grand reception and a pair of horses and carriage
You'll need determination, perseverance and courage
Neither is a bond created by material things
Life will throw many problems at you and it brings
both disasters and pleasures fit for kings
You have heard the saying, all work and no play
The next line might be, he or she will play away
Always ask your partner. What shall we do today?
It is not an easy path, mistakes not easily corrected
In times of stress you'll feel beleaguered, tested
Be calm and settle arguments when you are rested.

PART 3

NATURE ENVIRONMENT & HUMANITY

TURF WARS

With Global Warming
there are too many people
So, immigrants, wars.

Senryu

THE BARLEY MOW

There are many public houses in England named THE BARLEY MOW and nearly everybody will pronounce the mow in the same way as mow(to cut the grass), including me. But there is a much more interesting answer.

'THE BARLEY MOW' the word mow should be or was pronounced as in 'cow'. Barley which is used in beer production was not mown but reaped, originally with a sickle or scythe and tied into a sheaf. The heads of grain were then tied with twine so that the heads were at an angle and therefore the butts, meaning the bottom were also at an angle. This enabled the sheaf to lean inwards with all the butts resting on the ground when stood up to dry and the heads of grain facing outwards. Then the sheaves were stacked into stooks.

A STOOK, would consist of four to eight sheaves stacked so that they leaned against each other with the heads together and the butts on the ground, enabling the wind to pass through the stalks. If you look at an old painting or photograph of stooks you will notice that the air vent between the sheaves will be running North-South to enable the sun and wind to dry the grain.

A MOW. If the weather threatened to remain wet, the Stooks were stacked into a mini-rick of eight Stooks until it was dry enough to stack into a full sized Rick This was called a MOW.

There was a danger of spontaneous combustion if the Stooks were put into a stack when not dry enough.

A RICK. As a child we called a Rick, a Hay-Stack or Hay-Rick. So the Mini-Rick of eight Stooks was called a MOW rhyming with Cow or Plough.

SPRING

Time to forget those winter winds and icy cold
Spring means renewal and fresh colour to me
Watching for snowdrops to emerge, crocus unfold

As my lawns start to grow into velvet green
Daises poke up their heads as if to cheer
Elegant roe deer in two's, start to be seen

I see a seagull paddle his feet on the ground
imitating the sound of raindrops, then catching
worm's that rise up for fear of being drowned

Shaking the winters lethargy from our bones
I prune trees and see the fruit tree buds emerge
And we start to spring clean our homes

Then in the hope of hot summer sun
prepare for barbecues, and parties, looking
forward to inviting family, friends, everyone.

Note. This was my first attempt at an English Sonnet.

WHITE LIES

Being generous truthful and honest
Most often totally and badly backfires
Because people just cannot believe it
Then accuse you of being thieves and liar's

I tried my best to be truthful and generous
It did not work. That's where the problem lies
No matter how much money or aid is given.
Better to avoid the truth, if must, tell white lies

No matter how much food or help is given
because 'YOU CAN', by individuals, or Nation
Take care, it often it ends in accusations
of self-interest. Resulting in anger and indignation

Sadly; all my life I have seen, recipients
of charity with a wide smile. 'Wish you well'
but after receiving houses and State benefits
then wish for you to, 'Burn in Hell'.

Like the French revolutionaries did despise
all those with any sign of wealth
They were offered cake to eat, big mistake
Many heads were cut off, that's bad for health

Twisted minds often think that all donors
are lucky 'B's that won the lottery of life
My experience is that most; have worked hard
and often suffered deprivation and strife.

HAVE A NICE DAY

We all dream and wish
for the pristine beach
with clear clean water
and to eat fresh fish
But it is totally out of reach
for the majority of people
on this once wonderful clean world
Except for politicians, and nouveau riche.

Lone couples cavort on the white sand
Eat lobster with background of blue sea
This is what adverts continue to show
to the music of a local blues band
But when you have travelled
you soon will have learnt to know
The beach is muddy, the sea polluted
and all those travel plans, unravelled

Divide and rule. Image was the norm
Broadcasts used to control a nation
Television news used, to misinform
With pressure from governments view
programs have a bias, more or less
Politicians wanting re-election, a motley crew
News is often inconsequential claptrap
Newspapers under control of big business

Journalists seeking truth, take the rap
Man, and woman will always fight for more
Wealth can never be uniformly distributed
So sadly I say. This world is rotten to the core.

BE VERY SCARED

Humans will self-destruct in war
Sadly, it is in our nature
It's no use hoping for peace any more
Just look back at our history
Men and women will always fight
for rights, water, food and territory

When a country is dictated to by the army
and has rockets and nuclear weapons
controlled in the name of one party
Three minutes silence in six degrees below
No-one moves, talks or lifts their head
Nobody dares to move, it's a choreographed show

If you see everyone standing; so very still
when asked or ordered to do so
Reasoning says, there is no free will
Not one person has an adverse opinion
Because if they want to eat
they must be totally subservient, a minion

Everyone has reason to worry and be scared
Look at European history, and you'll find the
same reasons for suffering and Millions dead.

Note.
I saw on TV the North Koreans standing still in rank and file in minus 6 degree chill.

DREAMS

Dreams of Ivory towers and clean blue sea
Shiny new cars, Mall's with indoor snow to ski
150mph big cars which are just for show
With speed cameras there is nowhere to go

Gin palace yachts full of model's, ship ahoy
Sail away to avoid the common herd, the Hoy polloi
Lots of yachts don't go to sea, just sit and rust
in the salty yacht basins of the upper crust

Man is destructive, he pollutes the air, the sea
He is a predator. Yes, that includes you and me
The Chinese can see the minerals, the potential
their expansion in Africa will be exponential

Unfortunately now for the likes of you and me
The world is a such a dangerous place to be
Unless you're in a government position with
police and army protection, or sailing the sea

GREECE

Thinking of the Debt
Greece might be a Russian Port
Grease my palm or else

Haiku.

GREENBACKS AND BROWN PAPER

It is just a new name, Quantitative Easing
Printing money without the gold
It causes inflation, it is not pleasing
It's a fancy name, it's a game just the same,
In 1960 our house cost £2,200 pounds
Our lodger, a salesman called Rodger
purchased an E type jaguar to do his rounds

A case of the elite and you and me
Then a postage stamp or cup of tea
cost three old pence and
only one penny for a pee
There's a correlation, you will see
Now it's 2012 you will pay more
£180,000 for an average house
A top range car has this price; I'm sure
Many houses much higher I expect

Governments will keep Quantitative Easing here
Germans printed paper money in the war
like ticker tape, but that was small beer
Our children will have to get used to it
Youth have plenty to worry about and fear
Paying for third world Country bail-outs
and inflation makes our kids future unclear
caused by printing money, without assets.

Note. Greenbacks were renowned for being a safe currency, and the British pound was safe until PM. Brown sold all the gold. Brown paper used to be called bum paper (toilet paper) when I was a child.

DEAR LEADER

Standing silently in the winter chill
when asked or ordered to do so
Reasoning says, there is no free will

Not one person has an adverse opinion
If they want to live and want to eat
they must be totally subservient, a minion

Everyone has reason to worry of ruffians
Look at European history, and you'll find
Polish Officers suffered under the Russians.

FINITE WORLD

How many people can you fit in a phone box
How many can you cram into a car
How many can you pile up in to the sky

How many sheep can you keep in an acre
How many heifers can you feed from hectare
How many people can be fed on hundred hectares

Now think, you are living in a finite space
People will not shrink but they can starve
and the population is exploding rapidly,

Note Global Warming will also reduce the world food production.

CARBON TRAILS

A Supermarket has this sign
Every little helps
That sounds, just fine

Caring for the environment
Energy Efficient hand dryers
to help reduce our carbon footprint

But they buy and fly
Blueberries from Argentina
Leaving carbon trails across the sky.

WATER WARS

Only 2.5 per cent of World water is fresh
0.1 per cent is drinkable, at a guess
60 per cent of that fresh water lies
In ten countries that control supplies
Most of that fresh water is in Tibet
China rules there, the World will regret.
Africa and the Middle East
of water, they have the least.

Note. Desalination is too expensive for most Nations Countries that don't have sufficient fresh water or a sea must rely on keeping good relations with neighbouring countries.

SIEGE MENTALITY

If under a siege
You would tunnel for supplies
medicine and food

Haiku. Ref GAZA.

TURF WARS

With global warming
there are too many people
So, wars, immigrants.

Senryu.

Note. Regarding this next poem of mine called The Population Explosion.

I will explain why I wrote it, the sustainable level of human occupation is about 2 billion. There are now about 7 Billion and it is rapidly expanding. While at the same time resources are diminishing.

An Asteroid crashing into earth is required to change all that or a pandemic. I think that with over-crowding and fighting for resources it will result in a World Wide War

THE POPULATION EXPLOSION

Our Earth has a thin veneer, not all is habitable
Only part of its land mass is productive and liveable
that can provide safe shelter, food and water
All species eventually outgrow their space
and that applies to the human race
Politics call for greater growth
It's too late for our species
living in rubbish, faeces
Far too many people
It's unsustainable
and unstoppable
Armageddon
is soon
Boom
FIN

Note. This poem is in my first book but I repeat it as I feel it is an important message.

In 1946 at school a chart was shown to my class predicting the growth pattern for the world population.

It looked like what we now know looks like an atomic mushroom cloud. I was then 12 years old. It is an image that I never forgot.

SCHOOLING

The children of the Palestine Nation
require shelter, food and education

It is not the responsibility of the UN
and it's a possibility when they become men

If they cannot improve their life
the youth are likely to create more strife

And might want to punish their occupiers
with individual attacks bombs and fires.

OUR WORLD

As the polar ice completes its thaw
We are told that twenty kilometres of land
will be under the sea, then a there will be
a hundred million people displaced or more
The world was once clean, now I despair
What I see around me is now in decline
water shortages, bad air quality, rising sea
It's not renewable; it is in a state of disrepair

Note. A perpetual time machine, you might think, it is not as the dish will quickly fill.

All space will be taken and Countries will fight for all and any asset within their reach. Even the Arctic, deepest depths of the sea and even the Moon.

SNOWFLAKES EQUALS EARTHQUAKES

Snow what miracles you do perform
but you do not take the world by storm
These tasks are done by gentle persuasion
Take care, it is not soft on every occasion

Snow lands with a touch so light
often in the dark, long winter night
We awake to something we cannot understand
we fear, look and listen, it is quiet across the land

We have become used to constant sound
aircraft above, cars, lorries, rumble across the ground
When suddenly there is no noise, reaching our ears
it takes a little time to equate, to quell our fears

Then when the child and the child in me
see the white expanse, 'Snow' we shout with glee
When young, have you rolled naked in the snow?
then quickly ran into the house with healthy glow

Now when older, when blood runs slow
Desist, resist, just let the youngsters go
Wild animals and birds, do not have the same delight
it can cause starvation, finding food, a constant fight

Softly, softly, gently touching, building deep
at first the fluffy feel, easy to move, to sweep
it freezes into solid piles, like prisons

What is not seen is the weight it can create
it crushes roofs to devastate, avalanches suffocate

The first signs of the weight it has, mass
electric cables snap, trees come down, crash

The willow tree has got a solution
it learnt to bend by evolution
I have a tale to tell, it will make you shake
lack of snow, is the reason for the Haiti Quake

The world of ice and snow, the Polar Poles
have reason to be there, they have roles
Their part is to control the weather
and the ocean currents, now that is clever

The Earth is a balloon with a heavy ice crown
The ice, miles thick, is pressing down
Allow the ice to disappear, to melt
and the balloon will adjust, it will be felt

The Pole area will rise up, move and lift
This action will cause Tectonic plates to shift
that is why we now have so many quakes
Global warming, man's ineptitude is what it takes.

Note. I wrote the poem called Snowflakes Equals Earthquakes on 21/1/2010 and was surprised to find that on 2/7/2010 a science program on TV stated that Glacier's ice melting increases volcanic activity. I believe its technical name is Post-glacial rebound. Also on TV the 28/05/15 Secrets of the Earth seismologists said that large reservoirs cause stress on faults by the waters mass depressing the earth's crust (North West Research).But this effect is nothing compared to the relief of pressure by the melting of the glaciers and polar ice-cap with global warming, which will result in the earth's crust re-adjusting its equilibrium.
This coupled with the rising sea levels which will also alter the earth's delicate balancing act. Expect Earthquakes.

MONGOL TACTICS

Speed, mobility, hatred, systematic destruction
Street by street, block by block, total demolition

Square metre by square metre, tree by tree
leaving a desert as far as the eye can see.

Access, asset acquisition starvation, brutality, fear
All done without a care of a mother or child's tear

Control of food and water, power and aggravation
Deprivation, weakening the will of the population

Assets removed and sold including machinery
Banks controlled, trading in shares and currency

Hatred, jealousy, envy and greed are drilled
to have the required killer mentality instilled.

EMIGRATION

People in poverty
due to global warming
Which way? North is best.

Desert sands are expanding.

BILLY LIAR

Billy liar, all he said was lies
He was clever but quite ill
He did not understand truth
his only interest was oil supplies

When his ship did founder
in shallow sandbank water
Full of lethal jelly-fish
Declaring, "My voice is louder"

He climbed the vessels tall mast
and shouted from the crow's nest
"I will keep watch over you all
down there, while you last."

He unlike Blythe, his ship gone
his safety boat he then did sink
Sharks then did eat all his crew
But he kept swimming on and on

He had no need for any haste
He had protection, so blithely swam
The sharks around him did not like
his toothy grin and bitter taste

To foreign lands he always flies
as he no longer has a ship
Wheeling dealing, talking hawking
his business deals he plies.

Note. Captain Blythe (Mutiny on the Bounty) saved his crewmen by sailing a small boat 6,500 km across the Pacific Ocean.

YOU CAN ENTITLE THIS

They thought it just and right to chase
to persecute, and prosecute Saddam Hussein

Now they help the Kurds to fight for
independence with no financial gain

Unless, later there could be benefits from
owning shares in the Kurdish oil gravy train.

NIGHT Senryu

A quiet dark night
the sentry silently smokes
Bullet stubs his life.

PETROL BOMBS. Senryu

Why do police seem
to tolerate petrol bombs
They can kill people.

BOMBS

Secular States
Peace-full integration required
Bombs explode every day.

Senryu

SAVE EARTH ARMY

I served two years Army National Service
It actually did me some good
Now, I think, all school leavers should

And be taught their world is being degraded
What we need is a Save Earth Army
Now you will call me really barmy

The young are sheltered from the truth
That the world is in a perilous filthy state
Only seeing holiday places that countries create

They need to see the polluted rivers
Shanty towns, harbours full of oil and mess
Industrial areas with people living under duress

Save Earth Army conscripts would
See the truth, build with resolve and courage
be set tasks to try and repair the damage

Create goodwill, instead of waging war
with soldiers and the supply of arms
Improve living standards with all those healthy arms.

Note.
The oceans are producing more than half of the oxygen in the atmosphere and it absorbs the most carbon. Greenhouse gases are increasing acidity levels in the sea. Plastic pollution is killing many marine creatures and chemicals and oils are also killing or changing their body chemistry. If you want to eat fish you had all better be thinking about getting motivated.

Note. I was an advocate of joining the British Army. But I have changed my mind as our soldiers are taught to fight and when necessary kill but then they are persecuted as killers and receive no backing at all from their officers or government. 10/01/2016

HOUSE AND MONEY

Is there anywhere I can get a house and money?
Health care, Schools for free gratis without working
My belief there is no-where in this world
Apart from the UK, land of milk and honey
Just walk through the Channel Tunnel and it is all
yours including free National Health Services.

LAWRENCE OF ARABIA

Lawrence of Arabia
tried to create the perfect Arab garden
He was their hero like Bin Laden
A man with a dream, soldier, dissident or
politician's scapegoat? How was he seen
Was he honest or regarded as unclean

Initially empowered with true belief
in a cause, hoping for lasting peace
Coercion by politics would never cease
Things have not changed over the years
Arab tribes couldn't agree then or now
They cannot agree, for oil is the sacred cow

Note. I enjoyed reading his books.

FEAR

Who is going to build a town every year?
It will be Britain's responsibility I fear.
This will be needed to accommodate
migrants coming through Italy's open gate
Economic migrants from all over Africa
that put to sea, are taken to Lampedusa

Then a train trip to wait in a Calais tent
This will cause distress anger and dissent
They wait to stow away in any way, to Britain
Housing is given there without work or strain
Who will pay the bill? The British taxpayer will
Politicians will feel it. The voters won't stay still

Ebola is the predicted world pandemic
African hospitals are closing to the sick
Ebola will speed across Africa and the Med
as people run from the sick dying and dead.
There will be more and more young emigrants
leaving the old the dying and dependants.
2014.

BIRTH RATE

African birth rate
is the highest in the world
So they, immigrate

Senryu

AFRICAN ANGST.

Africa suffers war and depredation
There will always be deprivation
A splendiferous continent being spoiled
There are too many people in this world

Those with strong will, will prevail
The weak will fall and die on the trail
Who pays for all those guns and RPG's
that children carry and kill with ease

Man is destructive he pollutes the air, the sea
He is a predator. Yes, that includes you and me
The Chinese can see the minerals, the potential
Their expansion in Africa will be exponential

IF WE CAN'T WHY CAN THEY ?

Why is the UK so generous, so easily seduced
Family on holiday visa, she heavily pregnant
had their baby on the NHS within a month
while Schools and NHS funds, drastically reduced

Arrived destitute from South Africa, got a house
never ever worked or paid taxes here
No qualifications to tempt employment
Some pensioners here are poor as a mouse

My nephew waited on Council list for years
These visitors, within three months,
were ensconced in a Surrey Council house
It will all end in anger and many tears.

PIRATES

Pirates seem to control the sea
immigrate smugglers would agree
that Navies are unable to cope
that is plain for all of us to see

Pirates prey on people and possessions
they were hung drawn and quartered
unless they had permission from
Kings or Queens piratical concessions

Let ships arm themselves to fight
these bandits of the oceans
as soon as a threat is perceived
Protecting the pirates is not right

Very soon they will feel invincible
are there nations they do not touch?
Next they will target cruise liners
passengers on them are vulnerable

Don't think ransoms are for bread and honey
You will be told of their poverty but that's
no good reason to attack our ships
Guns will be bought with ransom money

BG.2009.

MORE IS LESS

Politicians, Industrialists cry
    "More is better, More production"
More immigration, more jobs so
    more taxation and consumption

Scientists and Military want to conquer space
Why? It is a very expensive type of race
Politicians know immigration control is lax
they only want a growth economy, to tax
The world is too small for the expanding human race
increasing temperature means new deserted space

The world will not remain gentle and temperate
People in deserts will move out or dehydrate
Others will drown in rising seas, low lying land
or die in tropical storms and mudslide sand
Countries are already drowning in water, I'm told
others so dry, water is worth more than gold

There are many signs that do indicate
friends will turn on each other in hate
You will fight, when food and oil are short
already millions require help and support
The Chinese decreed with wisdom and foresight
One marriage, one child, positive they are right

People protest about terminating pregnancy, abortion
Problems will be, food and water, how to apportion
the shrinking assets of food, water and living space
Also energy in this shrinking, stinking, finite place
Most problems caused by man's desire for growth
wealth, children, more space, you can't have both

In times of plenty, and international trade
Gifts of money and food are made
Beware, in drought and when harvests fail
and natural and man-made disasters prevail
When Russia has loses its harvest of grain
they stop exports, its own people to sustain

Prices will rise, shutters drawn, supplies cease
the poor will suffer, starve, catch disease
Countries will hold their stocks for themselves
quickly supermarkets will have empty shelves
The weather will increase the immigrants flight
fleeing their homelands when ethnic groups fight

Parts of earth are covered in ice or too low
too wet or too dry for crops to grow
Mountains too high and concrete covered cities
land that will be covered by the rising seas
We must all learn to live within our means
or subsist on desalinated water and beans

Author Notes
This was written in 2015. The World is not going to get any bigger and with the population expanding at the current rate there will be war, natural disaster or a pandemic to correct the situation.

FUTURE

We are mortgaging
the future of our children
by our consumption.

THE OVERLOADED DINGHY

If you were in a rubber dinghy
full of young people, out at sea

And others in a similar plight
had sank and with painful plea

They cry "Help please save us all."
as they all swam in the icy sea

But if you took just one child
you would all sink very quickly

So would you show you care
and then join them in eternity

Or would you practice self-preservation
and row away to re-join civilization?

Note.
This needs careful thought as there is a strong in-built sense of self-preservation in all of us.

POWER

I could hit you hard
with my fist, but if I missed
Better use writing.

Haiku.

THE NEW TIBET

Zimbabwe has accepted the Chinese Yuan
as its currency. Don't ignore this or yawn

Now its farmers must pay a land tax
China will rule as Zimbabwean's relax

Note.
The countries present leaders will gradually lose their role as the Chinese money men assume all control through the operation of railways and construction.

GRAFFITI

When graffiti is all you see
It is not a place to live or be
For dull minds are living there
In a state of deep despair
Pen and paper or the internet
Is a much better bet
For a way to express feelings
to other human beings
They endlessly repeat their sign
calling out. This place is mine
Like a mating call of a toad
By this, other gangs they goad
Perhaps it is better to have tattoos
So to recognize other crews
They feel deprived, perhaps justifiably
Their message being, don't Dis me.

Note. 'Dis me.' Means do not dismiss me.

OUR WORLD

Earth can only support so much life
Man and woman are smothering
covering the productive land
This will bring starvation and strife
Palm Oil plantations in straight lines drive
across the small farms valleys and hills
that was once productive countryside
Now only rats and snakes will survive.
Palm oil is being invested in heavily.

Note. Palm oil is a big industry in the Far East.

MODERN GOLD RUSH

Millions in North Africa need feeding, I am told
Aid makes them think, Europe is paved of gold
Millions are homeless in Sudan and Darfur
Pirates help themselves, what's the Navy for?
Western countries cannot keep an open door
to those that suffer deprivation and fleeing war
The answer lies in new farming techniques, education
Water control, conservation and less procreation

SUICIDE?

ISIS child bomber
Ten year old girl, suicide?
More like a murder.

Senryu

BREEDING DISCONTENT

Be "GREEN" and buy a tree, for a certain fee
spent to cut down jungle for the oil palm tree
The date palm plantations kill diversity
Save the Arctic wilderness, don't let it spoil
But gold is at $1600, for that miners will toil
Spoil detritus from that and drilling from oil?

In Africa, UN tented camps, women still breed
a desire to increase their brood, a basic need
This means there will be ever more to feed
It's been proven that charity money given for aid
has gone on guns to fight, when foreigners invade
So much more stringent measures must be made

Now empty your pockets to explore outer space
But it's all part of the military armament race
ready for when our earth blows up without trace
Outer Space, once a pristine place, with a view
to increase the human race, by a select few
Dream and scheme, I'm sure it will not be you

You are confined to your allotted tiny space
the population increasing at tremendous pace
until the military, not God will remove all trace
Thirty years exploration, now will turn to rust
For what result? to question this is a must
Was the cost of value? While Africa turns to dust

GROWTH WILL KILL

Politicians advocate growth and production
Too much will mean the end of every nation

The growth explosion of the human species
means that humans will empty all the sea's

Japanese will utilize all the types of whales
when large fish is already in short supply fails

Sharks are going for shark-fin soup by Chinese
When they're gone they will eat anything in the seas

Easter Islanders outgrew their finite space
Empty sea's will mean the end of the human race.

Look at recent history if you don't believe me
Africa's Lake Victoria, and shrinking Aral sea

There is a severe shortage of water in Botswana
you will find that that is the case in North Africa

People have started moving for a better life
Overpopulation will cause anger and strife

Barriers will get higher and harder to climb
The poor will starve while the rich buy time

You'll see those big yachts are Fall-out proof
to get away from the common herd ,to remain aloof

Avoid the populace, and hide on the ocean
to miss any rockets and nuclear explosion.

HUMANITY

When a soldier decides to lay down his life
in a thoughtful decision he alone did make
He laid down his life, he was so brave and kind
Medals are then given in order to remind mankind

When your dog has lost the use
of its hind legs, with ageing
and pleads silently with its eyes
Vets humanely put it down, to be kind

When a racehorse breaks a leg
financial decisions often apply
and humans will then often say
Best we put it down, to be kind

Murderers are given a lethal cocktail
to ensure a painless drift off to sleep
The law says they deserve a humane death
The law often behaves like an ass, I find

When a human is suffering lock-in syndrome acute
pain or paralysed and pleads to die, understanding the
anxiety of the close family around. Supposedly humane
humans say "Oh, No." They are stupid and blind.

Note. Tony Nicklinson a UK resident suffered from Lock-in syndrome. He went to the high court to ask to die humanely. It was refused. A few days later he died with a broken heart and after refusing to eat or drink. Is that humane? His last words were, "Goodbye world, I have had some fun."

I had a friend that asked my advice on suicide. I persuaded him not to do it. Ten days later he collapsed with lock-in syndrome and suffered a long slow mentally painful death. I know because he communicated with me with his eyelids.

TEARS AND FEARS

When people stand still in orderly rank and file
Bowing heads and crying out in dramatic style
All with carefully contorted face, but hardly a tear
All for the late Kim Jong-il. If not they'd disappear
When a country is dictated to by the army
and is controlled in the name of one party
Three minutes silence in six degrees below
Nobody dares to move, it's a choreographed show
When President John Kennedy died
Without outward show; I quietly cried
There was no need to show my grief
My quiet tears gave my anguish relief

This shows that there is something to fear in the country of North Korea.

POLLUTION

Every bit saved helps
Reduce our carbon footprint
Don't fly fruit and veg

Note. Haiku, the first two lines were in a supermarket advert.

269

A PIE IN THE SKY

Earth is an island from a spacecraft's view
Too many babies, that's people. Take note
An island can only constantly feed a few
Politicians always pat the baby's head
If anti-abortion and anti-contraception
do not change their thinking, many will be dead
There is a food shortage now, don't you know
People are starving right now, it will be worse
Nothing can continually expand and grow
Politicians have ships or super-yacht
They are havens in a crisis with crew
and stock of food and fuel, waiting for what?
Money can be made by short selling wheat
when the grain crops get ruined
Making profits when prices rise, that's neat
Wars and exploration of Mars cause me concern
let us settle for less, nothing grows forever
Why spend so much money on experiments like Cern
More growth, more jobs politician's cry, like a race
Do not join a race to ruin, Armageddon
Settle for less, less people, slow the pace
They pretend they can encourage growth
to get you all back to work, It's like
asking for speed record from a sloth
Easter Island population outgrew their isle
and ruined it by cutting all the trees
This, our island, our pie, ponder on it a while
The USA was nearly made bankrupt
by the Space and Moon landing programme, I pray
those you vote for, will not be stupid or corrupt.

ALL AT SEVENS

There are seven days in a week
Minimum seven days holiday we all seek

Every day is very much the same
But each day has a different name

Seven words in a poems rhyming line
Always sounds better than six or nine

Your short term memory holds seven units
They must be large, measured in Cubic's

The Seven seas described the World's Oceans
Also described the Oxus River by Persians

The Greeks thought seven plenty and perfection
They have often changed with people's perception

Clipper ships sailed East for China teas
Celebes, Flores, Java, Sulu, and Timor seas

Seven years marriage turns to an itch
The sweet loving lady becomes a bitch

Of all the Deadly Sins we are all so guilty
Lust, Greed, Sloth, Pride, Rath, Envy & Gluttony,

MORE IS LESS

More production more jobs, more immigration,
more consumption and more taxation
Scientists and Military want to conquer space
Why? It is a very expensive type of race
Politicians know immigration control is lax
they only want a growth economy, to tax
The world is too small for the expanding human race
Increasing temperature means new deserted space
the world will not remain gentle and temperate
People in deserts will move out or dehydrate
Others will drown in rising seas, low lying land
or die in tropical storms and mudslide sand
Countries are already drowning in water, I'm told
others so dry, water is worth more than gold
There are many signs that do indicate
friends will turn on each other in hate
You will fight when. food and oil are short
already millions require help and support
The Chinese decreed with wisdom and foresight
One marriage one child, positive they are right
People protest about terminating pregnancy, abortion
The problem will be, food and water, how to apportion
the shrinking assets of food, water and living space
and energy in this shrinking, fighting, finite place
problems caused by man & woman's desire for growth
More wealth, children, space, you cannot have both
In times of plenty, and international trade
donations of money and food are made
Beware, in drought and when harvests fail
and natural and man-made disasters prevail
When Russia has lost its harvest of grain
stopped exports, its own people to sustain
Prices will rise, shutters drawn, supplies cease
the poor will suffer, starve, catch disease

Borders will then be closed, walls then built
like North Korea, Israel, no feeling of guilt
There are families that have lived on aid for years
bearing children in the camps without fears
Countries will hold their stocks for themselves
quickly supermarkets will have empty shelves
Five million immigrants add to France's poor
Four hundred Tamils knock on Canada's door
The weather will increase the immigrants flight
fleeing their homelands when ethnic groups fight

by Simpleton on Aug 13, 2010. © Bernard Green.

OBESITY AND EFFECT

OBESITY

I see more Easter egg shapes each day
It makes me sad, I have to say
When I see fat children, I feel despair
that the parents, do not seem to care
Children following parents, in procession pass
with a walk, waddling along like a ducks arse
obese children walking with a rocking motion
Nobody dare comment to avoid confrontation
A cursory look at their shopping basket
reveals why they will soon occupy a casket
Food that makes cooking redundant, easier
Bread, pies, Cola fizzy drinks and pizza
We all want our children to have long life
avoid illness and the Surgeon's knife
Sugar is a culprit, it affects the inner body
Triglycerides are altered, bad for everybody
Palm oil in pastry, chips and crisps is to blame
It tastes so nice and it's cheap. That is a shame
It is in 10% of products in the supermarket,
So returning to mums home cooking is my target

Author Notes
Check out, American Heart Association on triglyceride's. National Institute of Diabetic Digestive and Kidney Diseases on palm oil.

I was nine and a half stone at the age of 21 and got to 15 stone working in my café, I ended up having open-heart surgery and the recovery from that was the most painful experience of my entire life.

SWEET POISON

Westerners can eat 22tsps o sugar every day
which results in a lot of tooth decay
The biggest problem is obesity and diabetes
eating all those high fructose cakes and sweeties

A 12oz can of Cola has approx. 7tsps of sugar
It puts a tyre on your waist, you're not a car

You think yoghurt is healthy, it can't hurt
but there's 6tps of sugar in a 6oz yoghurt

Sugar is addictive; it can change your mood
you might be eating 20tsps a day in your food
The average person eats 70lbs of sugar per year
resulting in cases of obesity and diabetes I fear.

FEEDERS

Feeding a person until they cannot walk
rise from a bed or pass through a door
should be an offence under State law
Force feeding a goose for Pate de foie gras
is illegal in some countries and States
The feeder is at fault for the problem it creates
You would definitely be charged with neglect
if you starved your dog, partner, child or kin
because you liked them as just bone and skin.

Note. I saw a TV programme about a man that fed his wife to be seriously clinically obese because he liked to see her fat. But he was very slim and healthy.

THE COLOSSAL COUPLE

Like ancient skin bags full of water
A man a woman son and daughter
Waggling and wobbling with arms out-splayed
They drank tinned Cola as they slowly sashayed

His bulging belly billowing over baggy bags
and sail-like summer shirt to hide all that sags
He with protruding pot belly perambulating his
pendulous posterior in Pickwickian pantaloons

She with big busts bursting over a bulging belly
sizable sagging bulging bottom bouncing badly
Swaying side to side, arms akimbo they flirt .
she swings around in her stupendous saggy skirt

They order Large Cod, Double Chips, and mushy peas
After every mouthful cover it with salt, if you please
They eat as if it is meant to be a race
cramming, ramming food into their face

It's not these peoples fault they are getting obese
What makes you look like a slug, it's not disease
There are preservatives in all mass prepared foods
chemicals that can affect your body and moods

Mind you. Is it their fault? I think it is not
as it is people that health education forgot.

Note. A day at the sea-side.

BUMS AND TUMS

I really don't wish to be rude
why are there so many big bums
and wobbly tums? It's in the food.

"It is in my genes." They cry
and I think that they believe it
"I slim, then get fat again." They sigh.

Gastric bands are all the rage
Breast reduction, tummy tucks
The big girls are not yet on centre page.

Somewhere there is a chemical imbalance
or a damaging product in our food chain
that causes so many calls for the ambulance.

Artificial colours, hydrogenated fat, preservatives
flavouring, monosodium glutamate.
Everything wrapped in plastic, things like that.

Why is there little research? No slimming success
Why is nothing done to help stop growing fat
Because there is no money in selling less!

Some-where in mass produced food and drink
there are additives that affect our bodies.
Soon there will be a tax on body fat, I think.

Note.
Joanna Blythman states in her book SWALLOW THIS. 12/02/2015. High fructose corn syrup has now been identified as the key driver of the obesity epidemic in the U.S.

THE WADDLE

They walked with a waddle
their cheeks wiggle and wobble
Chewing and chomping in unison
Fat mum, fat daughter, fat son
holding potato crisps and cola in their hands
they will all soon be requiring gastric bands.

DREAMING

I had a night-mare
I dreamt my wife was ugly
I woke up. She is.

Don't tell her about this poem, it's our secret.

ROLY POLY'S

Roly-poly pudding and pie
Bouncing bellies and bulging busts
How long before they die?

Carrying Cola as they crunch crisps
frequently resting due to breathing
Also aching backs and slipped discs

Why is it that now we see
people getting bigger, fatter
In my youth it never used to be

Perhaps because cows have been bred
to have bigger udders
for more milk, by being unnaturally fed

To increase the farmers yield
they feed chemical hormones
and cows are no longer in a field

Note. The feed contains hormones which to increase their yield

HAIKU-LOVE GIVEN

Cradled in your hug
your warmth enfolds me
just a babe in arms

Poem by © anaisanais A-M Docherty.

RELEASE, RELIEF, RENEWAL

You can release that inner turmoil
We all miss that turning, hit the rut
get on the wrong road, dark clouds appear
Write, open up, untie that knot in your gut
When a person writes, and creates
a story, poem, prose or ode
it will show a state of mind
a mood, modus vivendi, mode
We are all subject to moody moods
Fits of utter madness or despair
Doubts, regrets, remorse are with us all
writing helps to sooth, and clear the air

!8/02/2010

DUST TO DUST

When you and I are turned to dust
This unfortunately becomes a must
with no brain in what is left of you and I

A million trillion years will pass easily by
Enjoy this journey; slow is better than direct
the destination might not be what you expect

BELIEF

If you can feel the suns heat
from an object so, so far away

If you have seen a child grow
from your seed to be an adult

If you can have a thought
which you can turn to speech

If you understand that stars explode
to create clouds of gas and dust

And can understand that you
are created from that Stellar dust

If you can dream of something
then it is possible for it to happen

Then you will understand
Why there is belief in God.

WINTER

North wind is blowing
I think when it is snowing
Time to hibernate.

THE LAST FLIGHT

When it's time for this body to lie still
Will the inner me, the soul be free to
soar silently over valley, plain and hill
Being motionless is not my idea of bliss
it gives me moments of anxious thought
as I won't be able to give my wife another kiss

I believe my dust will blow around and re-appear
not as a ghostly, transparent apparition
but re-cycled as a bird or perhaps a deer
While in melancholy state of mind
I think of soaring in the sky
Perhaps my form will be a different kind

Hopefully I'll be part of a bird, not a fly
and if not possible to be in full control
I could be a teardrop in a child's eye
So tread lightly, and treat the fields with care
Think when picking flowers or treading on
creatures underfoot, for I might be there.

Written 17th Dec/2009

BEAM ME UP

Don't put me in a box with golden handles
when my due time is up
Do not shut or lock me up
for I am phobic, claustrophobic
This is my wish, my burning desire
please send me up in smoke, in fire

You can't make lamps out of me
for I don't have any tattoos
for you to scalp and amuse
Do not preserve this soft watery parcel
in aspic, plastic, formaldehyde or ice
when old and dead, it's not very nice

I'd like to think, away from man's stink
that I will be free to float around.
I'm sure that parallel universes abound
And I hope it's not dark and dank
when my creator decides my time is up
like Star Trek Scottie I will say "Beam me up"

My Mother did, her spirit flew away
so peacefully. I have this silly dream
Like her, I'd like to ride up a sunbeam
The Doctor dashed, but I said, "It's OK"
Do you know I never cried
for my Mum, the day she died

The sunbeam was shining on her head
I'm in the hospital by her side
I felt her go, on that sunny ride
Things you make, build, create
are quickly lost, broken, gone
but memories are very long

Like a vapour in each other's mind
You, me, we, to be or not to be
a person is not what you see
You can visualize, all past times good and bad
Where letters, photos can disappear in strife
Memories will stay with you and beyond your life

In my mind are those times with Mum
when conversing over a cup of tea
telling secrets only known to her and me
I've had much excitement, dives and dashes
so spread my dust in the garden bower
Perhaps, I can come back as a fragrant flower.

THE LAST PAGE

Old age is like the last page in a book
You don't want the end, but you will look

I want to compose more poetry
Write a book, earn a nice fat fee

It's time to show appreciation to my wife
who has shared all my trouble and strife

DEATH

I am not going to 'Pass away'
or 'Sleep the long sleep' I'll be dead
Nor 'Resting in peace.' I'll be dust.
I don't want my remains lying around
an empty case just getting in the way.

I won't be having a "Long sleep in Eden
or joining angels to play the harp
I will be dead deceased, departed
cremated, gone and forgotten my
ashes spread in our gorgeous garden

I do not want to go more rotten and stink.
Hopefully my chemicals will be re-used in the
growth of a beautiful flower or a butterfly.
Can you imagine me as such a delightful thing?
Far from how many people view me now, I think.

THE LAST ACT, ON ME

My last act will be
to fertilize the garden
You may then pee on me.

Senryu

THE END BUT HOPEFULLY NOT THE END OF DISCUSSION AND DEBATE.

DUNCE OR DYSLEXIC.
ISBN 978-0-9576042-0-9 By Simpleton.

An autobiography which is about early parachuting and the development of the first Skydiving Club in the UK. (British Skydiving) Written by Bernard Green under his allpoetry.com pseudonym of Simpleton.

This book is available on Kindle e-books on Amazon also there is an Audio book for the blind from the Royal National Institute for Blind People.

ZEPPELINS THAT BOMBED LONDON
By Bernard. A. N. Green.
ISBN 978-0-9576042-2-3

This book explains the development of airships from British balloons after the discovery of lighter than air gas. Then the German development of wooden framed Airships and Aluminium framed Zeppelins to use for bombing missions. Also included is the story of the incredible generosity of Sir Charles Wakefield who created and gave 353 solid gold medals to the Gunners and Searchlight teams that shot down the L15 /LZ48 this being the very first Zeppelin to be shot down over London.

BUILDING THE KHUFU PYRAMID-SHEDDING NEW LIGHT.
By Bernard A. N. Green.
ISBN 978-0-9576042-4-7

Available on Kindle e-books on Amazon.

The author's thesis as to how the Egyptians managed to build and lift the extremely heavy construction materials to such heights and accuracy.

The author had thought about this subject for most of his life and was then fortunate to meet Professor Menno Gerkema of the Dept. of Chronobiology & Dept., of Science and Society, the Netherlands who encouraged him to prove the concept and publish.

MY WIFE AND CANCER
By Bernard Green.
ISBN 978-0-9576042-5-4

A true story to illustrate some of the fear, anger, and frustration when cancer has been diagnosed. Also the effect that it has on those around the sufferer.

PHOTO SECTION

1 ALDERSHOT LIDO SWIMMING POOL. 290
2 ARMY SERVICE. 291
3 WILMSLOW. 292
4 THE HANDBAG RESERVE. 293
5 SHOREHAM. 294
6 WITH A STUDENT 295
7 THE FLYING SQUIRREL WAS THE LOGO FOR THE BRITISH SKYDIVING CLUB 1960 296
   A GLIDING RODENT.(A RAT). 297
   CIRCULAR CHUTE. 297
8 BIGGIN HILL. 1960. 298
9 THE ORIGINAL B.P.A. EMBLEM 1961. 299
10 BPA HEADED NOTEPAPER. 300
11 FIRST MAGAZINE OF THE BPA. 1964. 301
12 I BLEW IT. 302
13 BRITISH SKYDIVING AMBULANCE 303
14 AMERICAN AIRFORCE BEAVER 304
15 PLYMOUTH AIR RALLY 305
16 JOHN MEACOCK AND BILL CATT 306
17 THE ROLLS ROYCE. 307
18 BALLOON FLIGHT OVER LONDON 308
19 FLYING OVER THE CITY OF LONDON. 309
20 FINANCIAL TIMES 310

21 ALEXANDRA PALACE. 311
22 CERTIFICATE OF MERIT. 312

PHOTOS

1 ALDERSHOT LIDO SWIMMING POOL
I don't know what I am marching into!
There were muddy waters ahead.

2 ARMY SERVICE

ROYAL ENGINEERS AT SOUTHWOOD CAMP, COVE,
FARNBOROUGH, HANTS.
CORPORAL GREEN, TRAINING OFFICER.
THIS WAS MY SQUAD OF RECRUITS NEARLY
ALL BEING UNHAPPY CONSCRIPTS.

STORY-ARMY DAYS /GILFINAN.

3 WILMSLOW

MY HOUSE AT RUNFOLD USED AS THE 1ST OFFICE OF THE BRITISH PARACHUTE ASSOCIATION

MY TRIUMPH TIGER 110 JHV 939. 1960.

I wish I had kept it. It's the motorbike I mean.

4 THE HANDBAG RESERVE

At this period in time the parachutist had to pull the handle of the reserve chute. Then gather handfuls of the parachute and throw it to the side. Then hope it did not tangle with the collapsed main chute streaming above you.

This GQ reserve parachute was a great idea but mine just would not work.

Note. The story is at page 14.

5 SHOREHAM

Mike Reilly, Les Boddy, Martin Griffiths and Fred Gayler with the beard.
Packing USA C/9 with Red and White panels.

6 WITH A STUDENT

At Shoreham aerodrome. Martin Griffiths watching. He became an airline pilot.

7 THE FLYING SQUIRREL WAS THE LOGO FOR THE BRITISH SKYDIVING CLUB. 1960.

A GLIDING RODENT (A RAT)

The first and largest club was at Thruxton near Andover Hampshire, where the Chief Instructor was myself. We operated the De Havilland Rapide Aircraft. G-AKNN.

The second was at Halfpenny Green Aerodrome near Bobbington Stourbridge, West Midlands. Where we operated the Thruxton Jackaroo which was a Tiger Moth converted to a four seater. Mike West was the Instructor. The third club was at Stapleford Aerodrome, Stapleford Tawney, Romford. Essex. Pat Slattery was Instructor.

There we hired the aircraft. Pat Slattery was a very keen skydiver and sportsman. I was very sad to learn years later that he skydived and scuba-dived the same day and died from the bends.

To those that have never heard of the Bends it is bubbles of air in the blood and is a very painful way to die.

CIRCULAR CHUTE.

Giving his friends great mirth
Plain chute, heels, bum, head
Pride hurt by un-forgiving earth

By Graham Spicer.

A short poem by and about Graham Spicer. He is a great friend and solves my computer prolems. He is Archivist for the BPA.

8 BIGGIN HILL. 1960.

I had a motor controlled Russian camera on my helmet. Story - A load of rubbish.

THE BRITISH SKYDIVING CLUB CARAVAN.
This was taken to Air-shows to advertise the club.
Inside were parachutes and equipment that the public could examine.

9 THE ORIGINAL B.P.A. EMBLEM 1961.

THIS WAS THE ORIGINAL EMBLEM FOR THE BRITISH PARACHUTE ASSOCIATION WHICH WAS DESIGNED AND DRAWN BY A PARACHUTIST NAMED FRED GAYLER.

FRED WAS A MEMBER OF THE BRITISH PARACHUTE CLUB WHICH WAS BASED AT FAIROKS AERODROME, NR WOKING, SURREY.

THIS CLUB WAS SPONSORED BY THE GQ PARACHUTE COMPANY OF WOKING AND THE CHIEF INSTRUCTOR/ PILOT WAS JIM BASNETT.

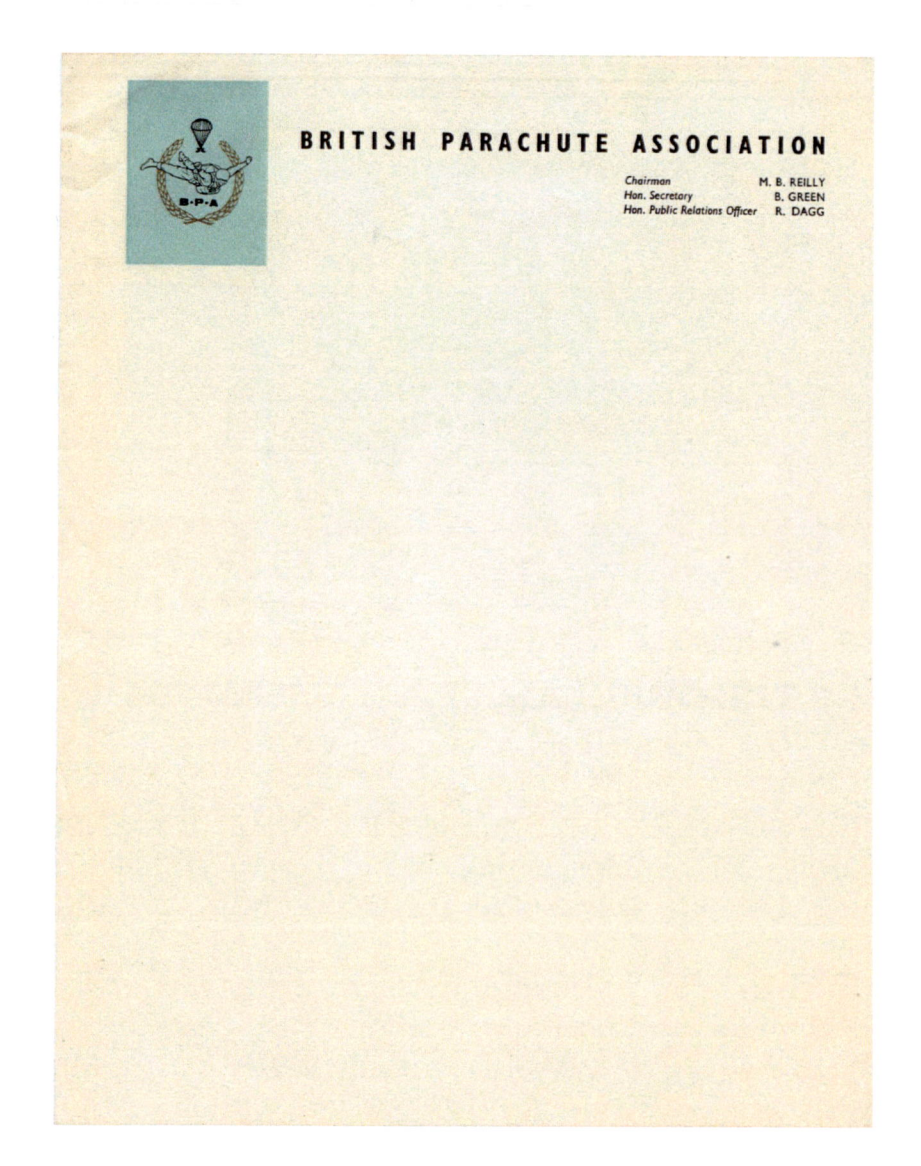

10 BPA HEADED NOTEPAPER

This was the original BPA notepaper with the excellent logo by Fred Gayler. 1961.

11 FIRST MAGAZINE OF THE BPA. 1964.

12 I BLEW IT

Descending on my first test jump, with this brand new GQ parachute. The second jump from high altitude blew it apart. This cut at the back of the chute was called a 7TU. That was the maximum you could cut out of the chute without the danger of it collapsing.

Note the front of the chute curling in.
The story is on page 50.

13 BRITISH SKYDIVING AMBULANCE

Also used for transport and kit. 18th Feb. 1962.
Look at the marvellous expanse of grass here at Thruxton and fields beyond the perimeter.

It was great fun driving the ambulance as everyone gave way to you at roundabouts and intersections.

14 AMERICAN AIRFORCE BEAVER

This aircraft flew Sherdy Vatsndal and myself to Mildenhall in Suffolk to give a skydiving display at their base. The following day after the show they flew us back to Fairoaks Aerodrome Woking

Sherdy Vatsndal is on the left of the picture.
He was superbly fit so it was strange that I was told that he died in bed of natural causes not many years later.

The story is *Skydiving in Style* on page 27.

15 PLYMOUTH AIR RALLY

DUNKESWELL AERODROME

On the left, Pat Slattery, next his good friend Des Smythe, 7th man is Sgt Mick Turner, 9th is myself, 12th is Sherdy Vatsndal. 13th Peter Lang,
I regret I cannot remember the other names.

16 JOHN MEACOCK AND BILL CATT

Standing in front of the British Skydiving Jackaroo aircraft at Thruxton. It was good up to 6,000ft with two parachutists on board.

They are wearing the American surplus kit that we were all using in the early 1960s.

B4 Harness with a C/9 rip-stop nylon 28ft canopy. Note the Capewell release system that enabled the release of the canopy in high winds or if landing in water. The British parachutes did not have these. The altimeters on the reserve packs were surplus wartime aircraft altimeters John Meacock eventually operated his own very successful Parachute Club.

17 THE ROLLS ROYCE

A 1962 James Young Silver Cloud. Aluminium body, a dividing partition and a cocktail cabinet inside.

It had the number plate SCT 100 which was the design number.

Story - The Funny Farm.

18 BALLOON FLIGHT OVER LONDON

13/03/1993. MY BALLOON. G-BURA.
THIS EVENT WAS ORGANIZED BY THE GREAT CHARITY THE VARIETY CLUB OF GREAT BRITAIN.

19 FLYING OVER THE CITY OF LONDON

Flying with me was Tim Bettin .Dr Geoff Boyes, Mike Andrews, and my elder son Alfred Bernard Green. I was going to land in a playing field behind a school in North London but had to negotiate over some trees. But my son shoved his nose to mine and shouted "Are you serious"

I changed my mind because the grass looked wet! No, he was correct it was risky! This meant we had a longer flight and landed in a large field at Potters Bar. As we left the field I saw a road named Tempest Avenue which was after 2nd Lt Wulstan J. Tempest.

20 FINANCIAL TIMES

DROPPING IN TO FLEET STREET

21 ALEXANDRA PALACE

OUR WONDERFUL VIEW. THE L31 ZEPPELIN.

I knew from writing about Zeppelins that in World War I that the L31 Zeppelin crashed at Potters Bar after being set on fire with incendiary bullets by 2nd Lieutenant Wulstan Tempest RFC on the 1st October 1916.

Captain Heinrich Mathy of the L31 decided to jump to his death rather than burn. All his eighteen crew were also killed. The loss of Mathy and the specially developed Zeppelin stealth bomber the L31 meant the end of Zeppelins and the concentration on larger faster aeroplanes.

Wulstan Park road entrance is where the L31 wreckage piled up against a large oak tree which is recorded on postcards of the time soon to be 100 years ago. This site is close to the Oakmere pool, Oakmere Park, Hertfordshire.

BRITISH PARACHUTE ASSOCIATION

Certificate of Merit

BERNARD GREEN

This is to certify that the above named has rendered a valuable service to the Sport of Parachuting.

The Chairman, Council and Members of the British Parachute Association are extremely grateful for this continued support of its activities.

Chairman

For your invaluable contribution and co-operation to the BPA Archive Project

National Coach & Safety Officer

Date 8th November 2013

22 CERTIFICATE OF MERIT

THIS CERTIFICATE WAS SENT TO ME ON THE 8TH NOVEMBER 2013.